Living in 1920s America

Myra Weatherly, *Book Editor*

Bruce Glassman, *Vice President*
Bonnie Szumski, *Publisher*
Helen Cothran, *Managing Editor*

GREENHAVEN PRESS
An imprint of Thomson Gale, a part of The Thomson Corporation

Detroit • New York • San Francisco • San Diego • New Haven, Conn.
Waterville, Maine • London • Munich

Cover credit: © Bettmann/CORBIS. Three young boys are entertained by an early radio program in 1921.
DigitalStock, 80
Library of Congress, 39, 56
National Archives, 10

LIBRARY OF CONGRESS CATALOGING-IN-PUBLICATION DATA

Living in 1920s America / Myra Weatherly, book editor.
    p. cm. — (Exploring cultural history)
  Includes bibliographical references and index.
  ISBN 0-7377-2801-9 (lib. : alk. paper)
    1. United States—Social life and customs—1918–1945. 2. United States—Social conditions—1918–1932. 3. Nineteen twenties. I. Weatherly, Myra. II. Series.
  E169.L778 2006
  973.91'5—dc22   2005050215

Contents

Chapter 3: Arts and Entertainment

such as New York. These private clubs were sometimes operated by gangsters eager to cheat the customers.

Foreword

T oo often, history books and teachers place an overemphasis on events and dates. Students learn that key births, battles, revolutions, coronations, and assassinations occurred in certain years. But when many centuries separate these happenings from the modern world, they can seem distant, disconnected, even irrelevant.

The reality is that today's society is *not* disconnected from the societies that preceded it. In fact, modern culture is a sort of melting pot of various aspects of life in past cultures. Over the course of centuries and millennia, one culture passed on some of its traditions, in the form of customs, habits, ideas, and beliefs, to another, which modified and built on them to fit its own needs. That culture then passed on its own version of the traditions to later cultures, including today's. Pieces of everyday life in past cultures survive in our own lives, therefore. And it is often these morsels of tradition, these survivals of tried and true past experience, that people most cherish, take comfort in, and look to for guidance. As the great English scholar and archaeologist Sir Leonard Woolley put it, "We cannot divorce ourselves from our past. We are always conscious of precedents . . . and we let experience shape our views and actions."

Thus, for example, Americans and the inhabitants of a number of other modern nations can pride themselves on living by the rule of law, educating their children in formal schools, expressing themselves in literature and art, and following the moral precepts of various religions and philosophies. Yet modern society did not invent the laws, schools, literature, art, religions, and philosophies that pervade it; rather, it inherited these things from previous cultures. "Time, the great destroyer, is also the great preserver," the late, noted thinker Herbert J. Muller once observed. "It has preserved . . . the immense accumulation of products, skills, styles, customs, institutions, and ideas that make the man on the American street indebted to all the peoples of history, including some who never saw a street." In this way, ancient Mesopotamia gave the world its first cities and literature; ancient Egypt, large-scale architecture; ancient Israel, the formative concepts of Judaism,

Christianity, and Islam; ancient Greece, democracy, the theater, Olympic sports, and magnificent ceramics; ancient China, gunpowder and exotic fabrics; ancient Rome and medieval England, their pioneering legal systems; Renaissance Italy, great painting and sculpture; Elizabethan England, the birth of modern drama; and colonial America, the formative environments of the founders of the United States, the most powerful and prosperous nation in world history. Only by looking back on those peoples and how they lived can modern society understand its roots.

Not all the products of cultural history have been so constructive, however. Most ancient Greeks severely restricted the civil rights and daily lives of women, for instance; the Romans kept and abused large numbers of slaves, as did many Americans in the years preceding the Civil War; and Nazi Germany and the Soviet Union curbed or suppressed freedom of speech, assembly, and religion. Examining these negative aspects of life in various past cultures helps to expose the origins of many of the social problems that exist today; it also reminds us of the ever-present potential for people to make mistakes and pursue misguided or destructive social and economic policies.

The books in the Greenhaven Press Exploring Cultural History series provide readers with the major highlights of life in human cultures from ancient times to the present. The family, home life, food and drink, women's duties and rights, childhood and education, arts and leisure, literacy and literature, roads and means of communications, slavery, religious beliefs, and more are examined in essays grouped by theme. The essays in each volume have been chosen for their readability and edited to manageable lengths. Many are primary sources. These original voices from a past culture echo through the corridors of time and give the volume a strong feeling of immediacy and authenticity. The other essays are by historians and other modern scholars who specialize in the culture in question. An annotated table of contents, chronology, and extensive bibliography broken down by theme add clarity and context. Thus, each volume in the Greenhaven Press Exploring Cultural History series opens a unique window through which readers can gaze into a distant time and place and eavesdrop on life in a long vanished culture.

Introduction

In the 1920s people living in the United States experienced an unprecedented period of technological development. For example, at the beginning of the decade, only 34.7 percent of American houses had electric power; by 1930, 67.9 percent of homes had electricity. Hot and cold running water also became increasingly common, especially in urban areas. "We . . . are probably living in one of the eras of greatest rapidity of change in the history of human institutions,"[1] concluded sociologists Robert S. Lynd and Helen M. Lynd in the mid-1920s. The impact of new technology affected the ideas, tastes, values, and behavior of American society. Three of the technological innovations of the 1920s that had the greatest impact on the way Americans lived were the automobile, radio, and cinema.

The Automobile Transforms America

Although gasoline-powered automobiles had been manufactured in the United States since the late nineteenth century, only the very wealthy had been able to afford them. In the 1920s, however, manufacturer Henry Ford introduced the assembly-line production of cars, which drove down their price so that millions of Americans could afford to buy one. By the late 1920s, there was one automobile for every five Americans. As professor of history David E. Kyvig writes:

> Gasoline-powered, internal-combustion-engine-propelled vehicles had been around for more than a quarter-century by the start of the 1920s, but not until that decade did they become a general factor in the everyday lives of ordinary Americans. Mass production, together with innovations in design, engineering, manufacture, and sales brought a new or used car, truck or tractor within reach of most people.[2]

The coming of the automobile age had a far-reaching effect on American life. One of the greatest changes was people's increased mobility. Men and women who previously might have married and never ventured far from the town they were born in were now able to travel greater geographical distances. Cars allowed them to visit new places and meet new people. Rural Americans were no longer isolated on their farms or in the country; instead, they could drive into towns and cities to work, shop, or be entertained.

The automobile also influenced the rituals of courtship in America. Before the 1920s, the custom was for a suitor to court a young woman by calling on her at her house, where the couple would socialize in the parlor under the close supervision of her parents. With the advent of the car, young people embraced a new social freedom. As historian Fon W. Boardman Jr. describes,

> In no area did the automobile bring about more change than in that of dating and courtship. Previously young couples had spent many hours in the home parlor; now the automobile became a parlor on wheels, taking them to more exciting places and away from parental supervision.[3]

The Effect of Radio on America

Like the automobile, the newly developed radio in the 1920s was a tool that broke down geographic boundaries in America and, as historian Tom Lewis notes, "drew people together as never before."[4] Radios were substantially cheaper than cars and soon became part of virtually every American home. People could listen to live broadcasts from towns and cities all around the country and experience events with an immediacy previously unavailable. On the night of November 2, 1920, station KDKA in East Pittsburgh broadcast the presidential election returns in the race between Warren G. Harding and James M. Cox as many Americans eagerly listened. Little more than a year later, an estimated 300,000 people heard the live radio broadcast of the heavyweight boxing championship match in which American Jack Dempsey defeated Frenchman Georges Carpentier.

The radio was the first modern tool of mass communication and gave people a new way to gather information and interact. It also allowed listeners to experience new ideas and entertainment and to form opinions on matters concerning the nation and world affairs. People stayed up late at night listening to the news, sports events, radio comedy, concerts, and sermons. "With radio, the people in the Midwest could listen to a concert in Boston, a

Beginning in the early 1920s, the radio allowed families to listen to programs from all over the country.

preacher in California, or President [Calvin] Coolidge in the White House, all from the comfort of their own living rooms,"[5] writes cultural historian Janet McDonnell. From the outset, music programs filled a great percentage of airtime. Operas and orchestral performances were frequently broadcast. Radio stations also promoted jazz and country music to many audiences experiencing these forms of music for the first time.

By providing people around the country with common access to the same kinds of information, education, and entertainment, the radio served as a means of uniting the nation in a way never before experienced. According to author Elizabeth Stevenson:

> Radio not only reported the events but shaped them. Radio strengthened a tendency already working to make people of the United States feel united and whole. For the first time, it seemed as if they could have thoughts and feelings simultaneously.[6]

The Impact of Movies on American Popular Culture

Like the radio, the cinema became an enormously popular source of mass entertainment during the 1920s. By the end of the decade, three-fourths of Americans went to the movie theater every week, and there were twenty Hollywood studios. In fact, the American film industry was most productive in the 1920s and 1930s, releasing an average of eight hundred films a year.

The popularity of movies featuring glamorous and sophisticated actors and actresses greatly shaped popular culture. Thousands of young women followed the fashion fads fueled by the silver screen. Young men were enthralled by the new adventures and dramas and were influenced by the style of their favorite movie heroes. As millions of Americans from all over the country watched movies in theaters ranging from the grand "picture palaces" to the plainest curtained rooms, they were exposed to new ideas and images on a grand scale. "Movies, as much or more than radio, served to break down provincialism, increase awareness of the unfamiliar, and create a national community with a specific set of shared experiences,"[7] states Kyvig.

Technology played a vital role in shaping the culture and economy of the 1920s. By the end of the decade, the automobile had created a more mobile society and blurred the distinctions between urban and rural America. In addition, a shared sense of taste, values, and behaviors communicated by radio and cinema contributed to the development of a common national culture. Proliferation of these two media gave Americans from all over the country the same opportunity to "listen to the same songs and speeches, laugh at the same jokes, and admire the same fashions,"[8] writes McDonnell.

Notes

1. Quoted in Nathan Miller, *New World Coming*. New York: Scribner, 2003, p. 172.

2. David E. Kyvig, *Daily Life in the United States, 1920–1939: Decades of Promise and Pain*. Westport, CT: Greenwood, 2002, p. 27.

3. Fon W. Boardman Jr., *America and the Jazz Age: A History of the 1920s*. New York: Random House, 1968.

4. Tom Lewis, "'A Godlike Presence': The Impact of Radio on the 1920s and 1930s," *OAH Magazine of History*, vol. 6, Spring 1992, p. 1.

5. Janet McDonnell, *America in the 20th Century*. New York: Marshall Cavendish, 2003, p. 358.

6. Elizabeth Stevenson, *The American 1920s*. New York: Macmillan, 1962, p. 114.

7. Kyvig, *Daily Life in the United States*, p. 91.

8. McDonnell, *America in the 20th Century*, p. 422.

Family and Society

CHAPTER
1

Chapter Preface

During the 1920s, American society embraced a new manner of living, fueled by the growing prosperity of the country, technological innovations, and cultural changes. Manufacturers were producing standardized products such as cars, radios, and refrigerators in unprecedented quantities. New and expanded industries created more jobs with higher salaries. The nation was also undergoing what historian Frederick Lewis Allen called "a revolution in morals" as the younger generation rejected the moral codes of their parents. Many young women bobbed their hair, wore short skirts, and were much more flirtatious and assertive than the demure women of the previous generation. These changes in the standard of living, the availability of goods, and the attitudes of young people all had a particularly profound impact on the lives of women and families.

By the time the decade began, women had gained the right to vote. By the mid-1920s, writes historian Lois W. Banner, "it had become a matter of belief—proclaimed by the press and radio, businessmen, and politicians—that women had in fact achieved liberation." The demand for workers during World War I had opened up employment opportunities for millions of women. Access to automobiles afforded women greater opportunities to work outside the home, often in jobs traditionally held by men. Women were also gaining entry to the previously male-only world of speakeasies, saloons, and golf courses. Although women still faced great inequality in many aspects of life, including wage discrimination, they were in fact making progress in many areas.

As the role of women changed in the 1920s, the American family also changed. The traditional structure of the family was transformed by a new ideal of family life called the "companionate family." According to this ideal, husbands and wives were expected to be companions rather than adhere to the traditional family hierarchy of a dominant father and subservient mother and children. The ideal of the companionate family, combined with a declining family size, resulted in children receiving more individual attention than in earlier times. Most mothers in the 1920s took the job of rearing their children seriously and wanted to do it the right way, following the advice of experts. As author Kim Klausner writes, "Some of the guiding principles of industrialization, particularly efficiency and time management, had infiltrated the home. Women were encouraged, and many attempted, to raise their children according to both scientific and managerial principles." And in their study of a typical small town in 1925, social anthropologists Robert S. Lynd and Helen M. Lynd observed that "one cannot talk with Middletown mothers without being continually impressed by the eagerness of many to lay hold of every available resource for help in training their children."

The years from the end of World War I to 1929 saw extraordinary economic growth and change for most Americans, but hardly all. Census data for the 1920s gathered by the U.S. Bureau of the Census classified between one-third and two-fifths of the American population as poor. Significant poverty characterized the lives of many farm families, who were unable to share in the higher standards of living enjoyed by much of the country. Nonetheless, the dramatic developments in technology, the workplace, and family life in the 1920s have contributed greatly to today's American culture.

Houses in a Small Town

Robert S. Lynd and Helen Merrell Lynd

In 1925 sociologists Robert S. Lynd and Helen Merrell Lynd explored the impact of modernization on everyday life in the small town of Muncie, Indiana, which they gave the fictitious name "Middletown" in their published work *Middletown: A Study in American Culture.* In their study the authors show how life has changed in Middletown from the 1890s to the 1920s, including the ways in which people earn a living, educate their children, spend their leisure time, and contribute to the community. In the following excerpt from their study, the Lynds examine the various kinds of housing that had been developed in Middletown by the 1920s. They note that the shabby, one-story wooden houses of the poorest working-class families had changed little since the middle of the nineteenth century. On the other hand, members of the upper class in the 1920s were building houses with "greater simplicity of line" than the elegant homes of the past. Some of these "modern" homes even had the luxury of central heating and running water. The Lynds point out that conveniences such as electric lighting and stoves, which only the very wealthy had been able to afford at the turn of the century, were now used by the majority of people in Middletown.

Robert S. Lynd served as professor of sociology at Columbia University, and Helen Merrell Lynd was a professor of social philosophy at Sarah Lawrence College. They are also the authors of *Middletown in Transition.*

The forty-three people in each hundred who get Middletown's living [i.e., who earn an income] divide their lives regularly between two places: their best walking energies, five and a half out of every seven days, are spent in the buildings set apart for industry and business; their other activities traditionally center

Robert S. Lynd and Helen Merrell Lynd, *Middletown: A Study in American Culture.* San Diego: Harcourt Brace Jovanovich, 1929.

about the homes in which they and their families sleep and eat. In these homes the twenty-three people in each hundred who are engaged in making the homes of the city, the four in each hundred who are the very old or feeble, the eleven who are very young, and, to a considerably less extent, the nineteen receiving required school training, carry on their respective activities. Next to the places where people get a living, these homes form the most apparent locus of the lives of the community.

Middletown's 38,000 people live in 9,200 homes: 86 per cent. of these homes are in one-family houses, each standing on a separate patch of ground, the latter called, with increasing significance in view of its shrinking size, "a yard"; 10 per cent. are in two-family houses, a more common type since 1890 as building costs have risen; 1 per cent. in apartments; and 3 per cent. over stores, chiefly in the "downtown" section. The life of a house in Middletown is thirty to fifty years, and, as in each new generation the less well-to-do tend to inherit the aging homes of the group slightly "better off" in the preceding generation, the city lives, in the main, in houses fifteen to forty years old. Although working class families tend to be larger than those of the business class (the 124 working class families interviewed average 5.4 members each and the forty business class families 4.7), it is the business group, generally speaking, who live in the larger dwellings; one in each three of the 124 working class families interviewed and four out of five of the forty business class families live in single-family houses large enough to have two floors.

In the [eighteen] eighties the usual size of the plot of ground on which a house was built was sixty-two and a half feet fronting on the street, with a depth of 125 feet; the standard building lot today has a frontage of forty feet. Whereas the city blocks of 1890 usually contained eight lots, the same blocks now contain ten, twelve, and even fourteen. A common practice today is to saw off the back of a lot and insert an additional house fronting on the side street. The implications of this shift for playroom for children, leisure-time activities for the entire family, family privacy, and even for the former sense of substantial pride in the appearance of one's "place" are obvious. Houses are crowding closer to the front paving-line, and flowers and shrubbery must give way as the lawn shrinks to allow a driveway to the garage. The housewife with leisure does not sit so much on the front porch in the afternoon after she "gets dressed up," sewing and "visiting" and comparing her yard with her neighbors', nor do the family and neighbors spend long summer evenings and Sunday afternoons on the porch or in the side yard since the advent of the automobile and the movies. These factors tend to make a decorative yard less urgent; the make of one's car is rivaling the looks of one's place as an evidence of one's "belonging."

Building Materials

Houses are usually built of wood. Those of the poorest working class families appear essentially the same externally as they did in the middle of the last [nineteenth] century—bare little one-story oblong wooden boxes with a roof and with partitions inside making two to four small rooms. At the other extreme are the large homes of the more prosperous members of the business class; these exhibit considerably greater simplicity of line than a generation ago, when an "elegant new residence" might be described in the press as a "conglomeration of gables, nooks, verandas, and balconies with three stone chimneys towering above, giving the appearance of an ancient castle."

Trends in Porches

In the eighties with their ample yards, porches were not urgently needed. Towards 1900, as smaller yards were driving the family closer to the house, people began to hear of porches in the state capital "fitted up like a room," and the era of porch furniture began; small wood-working plants that were losing their local trade in wagons and agricultural implements exploited this new specialty eagerly. Already, however, business class homes are leading the way in a reversion to porchless designs with glassed-in sun parlor and sleeping porch, the latter showing how far Middletown has moved from its "fear of the night air," which in 1890 prompted sleeping with windows down a gingerly six inches at the top. Today none of the workers' houses has a sleeping porch and relatively few of the homes of the business group, but according to a local building expert, "The man who puts $8,000 and up into a house today demands a sleeping porch." The trend is apparently to divert the money formerly put into front porches to sleeping porches, glassed-in dens, and other more private and more often used parts of the house.

A Middletown building expert estimates that the majority of homes constructed within the last ten to fifteen years have at least 50 per cent. more glass surface than in 1890. More air can be let in from without today because more heat can be secured within. Several hundred homes are heated by a central heating plant operated under city franchise and hundreds of others by furnace, steam or oil, although most of the working class still live in the base-burner and unheated-bed-room era. With furnaces have come basements which, in the sense of cement-floored and walled rooms beneath the house, were practically non-existent in the Middletown of 1890. This inconspicuous item of basement, plus foundation, adds $700 to the cost of even a small house; a basement today costs about what a small house cost in the early nineties.

Improvements in Plumbing and Electricity

There was no running water prior to 1885, and by 1890 not more than 20 per cent. of the total mileage of the city's streets was underlaid with water mains. It is estimated that in 1890 only about one family in six or eight had even the crudest running water—a hydrant in the yard or a faucet at the iron kitchen sink. A leading citizen thought it sufficiently important to enter in his diary in 1890 that a neighbor "has a hydrant for his house." The minutes of the Board of Education for 1888 contain an item: "Eph Smell . . . 1 wooden pump for High School . . . $10.00." For the most part, Middletown pumped its water to the back door or kitchen from a well or cistern. By 1890 there were not over two dozen complete bathrooms in the entire city. For approximately ninety-five families in each hundred, "taking a bath" meant lugging a heavy wooden or tin tub into a bedroom, or more usually the warm kitchen, and filling it half full of water from the pump, heated on the kitchen stove. Today all new houses, except the very cheapest, have bathrooms, and many old houses are installing this improvement rapidly. Many homes, however, still lack not only bathroom, but in January, 1925, approximately one in four of all the city's dwellings lacked running water. This considerable use of a water supply from back-yard wells accompanies the persistence in even more working class homes of the old-fashioned backyard "privy." According to the City Engineer, only two-thirds of the houses had sewer connections in 1924. It is not uncommon to observe 1890 and 1924 habits jostling along side by side in a family with primitive back-yard water or sewage habits, yet using an automobile, electric washer, electric iron, and vacuum cleaner. This unevenness in the diffusion of material culture becomes even more significant in the light of the community's public health service with its outwardly stringent prohibition upon back-yard water supplies and back-yard toilets and sewage disposal.

Electric lighting is so much a matter of course today that it is hard to recover the days before its advent. The Middletown press in 1895 regarded natural gas as the last word in homemaking—"the millennium of comfort and cleanliness is at hand"; but most of the discoveries and virtually all of the enormous popular diffusion of modern electricity in terms of the home—electric lighting of a brilliance and steadiness undreamed of then, labor-saving devices for cleaning the house, washing clothes, and cooking—still lay in the future. Over 95 per cent. of Middletown's houses were without electricity in 1890; by 1916, 60 per cent. were using electricity for lighting purposes, and in June, 1925, 99 per cent. of the homes were wired and presumably at least lighted by electricity. In slightly more than two out of each three families cooking is done with gas at the present time, the others using gasoline, coal, and a very few electricity.

Interior Plans

No other changes in Middletown's homes have been as marked as the adoption by the bulk of the community of these various conveniences, used only by a few of the very wealthy in the nineties. The interior plan of the house has remained fundamentally the same, although there has been some trend toward fewer and larger rooms, the "parlor" and the "spare bedroom" being the casualties. In some working class homes the parlor, living room, and kitchen have become living room, dining room, and kitchen, but in many the parlor survives, in which case the family lives in the dining room. Among the business class and in the case of the newer bungalows of the working class, the tendency is to throw together much of the lower floor by means of large double doorways.

The main type of interior furnishing, as well as of plan of house, is fairly definitely fixed in the habits of all groups; a higher standard of living exhibits itself, not in any radical departure from this general type, but in minor variations and more costly elaborations.

Typical House of the Poor

The poorer working man, coming home after his nine and a half hours on the job, walks up the frequently unpaved street, turns in at a bare yard littered with a rusty velocipede or worn-out automobile tires, opens a sagging door and enters the living room of his home. From this room the whole house is visible—the kitchen with table and floor swarming with flies and often strewn with bread crusts, orange skins, torn papers, and lumps of coal and wood; the bedrooms with soiled, heavy quilts falling off the beds. The worn green shades hanging down at a tipsy angle admit only a flecked half-light upon the ornate calendars or enlarged colored portraits of the children in heavy gilt frames tilted out at a precarious angle just below the ceiling. The whole interior is musty with stale odors of food, clothing, and tobacco. On the brown varnished shelf of the sideboard the wooden-backed family hair brush, with the baby bottle, a worn purse, and yesterday's newspaper, may be half stuffed out of sight behind a bright blue glass cake dish. Rust spots the base-burner. A baby in wet, dirty clothes crawls about the bare floor among the odd pieces of furniture.

Middle Class Homes

The working man with more money leeway may go home through a tidy front yard; whether his home is of the two-floor variety, a bungalow, or a cottage, there are often geraniums in the front windows, neat with their tan, tasseled shades and coarse lace curtains. A name-plate of silvered glass adorns the door. The small living room is light, with a rather hard brightness, from the blue- and pink-flowered rug, bought on installment, to the artificial flowers, elaborately embroidered pillows and many-colored "center pieces." The furniture is probably straight-lined "mission" of dark or golden oak or, if the family is more prosperous, "over-stuffed." The sewing machine stands in the living room or dining room, and the ironing board with its neat piles of clothes stretches across one corner of the kitchen. "Knickknacks" of all sorts are about—easeled portraits on piano or phonograph, a paper knife brought by some traveled relative from Yellowstone Park, pictures that the small daughter has drawn in school, or if the family is of a religious bent, colored mottoes: "What will you be doing when Jesus comes?" or "Prepare to meet thy God." There may even be a standing lamp with a bright silk shade, another recent installment purchase and a mark of prestige. Some magazines may be lying about, but rarely any books.

The homes of some head bookkeepers, owners of small retail stores, school teachers, and other less wealthy members of the business group convey an atmosphere of continual forced choices between things for the house and things for the children—between a hardwood floor for the front hall and living room or a much-needed rug and the same amount of money put into music lessons or Y.M.C.A. summer camp. These houses may be twenty years old and unadorned, with small rooms and a miscellany of used furniture. There is less likely to be a radio than in the more prosperous working class home, but one may come upon a copy of Whistler's portrait of his mother or a water-color landscape and a set of Dickens or Irving in a worn binding; the rugs are often more threadbare than those in the living room of a foreman, but text-books of a missionary society or of a study section of the Woman's Club are lying on the mission library table.

To some more prosperous members of the business group their homes are a source of pride as they walk up a neatly paved, tree-bordered street to homes which are "the last word in the up-to-date small house." The house may be shingled or stuccoed, in a trim terraced yard. Everything from the bittersweet in the flower-holder by the front door to the modern mahogany smoking table by the over-stuffed davenport bespeaks correctness. The long living room opens by a double doorway into the dining room. Colors in rugs, chair coverings, curtains, and the elaborate silk shades of the standing lamps match. There are three or four pictures—colored photographs or Maxfield Parrish prints—hung precisely at the level of the eyes, a pair of candle-sticks on the sectional bookcase, and a few bowls and trays; the kitchen cabinet has every convenience. Here one sees the complete small house. "It's so hard to know what to give our relatives for Christmas any more," said one woman; "they have their homes and their knick-knacks and their pictures just as we have. It's hard to find anything new that they haven't got. We've stopped giving to our friends except just cards, but we have to give to the family."

Houses of the Wealthy

A group of wealthy families live in "fine old places" in the "East End" of town, some of them still in the houses where the husband or wife was born. These houses may be large, heavy brick or stone affairs with perhaps two stone lions guarding the driveway near the old hitching post and carriage block bearing the owner's name. Other families live in rambling, comfortable frame houses in this section, while still others are following the movement out to the newer college district. Here they build low homes of brick or field stone or of the white Dutch colonial type with every convenience in the way of plumbing and lighting and with spacious glassed-in porches.

Whether the father of one of these families comes home from office or bank to the large parlors and library of the older type of house or to the ample long living room of the new, he is greeted by an atmosphere of quiet and space. The wide rooms, soft hangings, old mahogany, one-toned rugs or deep-colored Orientals, grand piano, fireplaces, cut flowers, open book-shelves with sets of Mark Twain and Eugene Field and standard modern novels, the walls hung with prints of the Bargello, St. Mark's, "Mme. Lebrun and Her Daughter" may be combined with certain individual touches, a piece of tapestry on the wall, a picture not seen elsewhere, a blue Chinese bowl.

Here, then, in this array of dwellings, ranging from the mean and cluttered to the spacious and restful, Middletown's most "sacred" institution, the family, works out its destiny. Within the privacy of these shabby or ambitious houses, marriage, birth, child-rearing, death, and the personal immensities of family life go forward. Here, too, as at so many other points, it is not so much these functional urgencies of life that determine how favorable this physical necessity shall be in a given case, but the extraneous detail of how much money the father earns.

Changes in Family life

David E. Kyvig

In the 1920s the daily lives of ordinary Americans changed in many ways. In the following selection, historian David E. Kyvig describes the transformation in the way families lived, including the dating practices of teenagers. The social ritual of courtship moved from the family parlor to the family car as young people sought greater privacy and freedom from adult supervision. This use of the family automobile for dating became a source of tension between parents and teenagers, Kyvig notes. He also points out that divorce rates skyrocketed during the 1920s and remarriage became more common as people began to seek greater emotional fulfillment in marriage. Health care also underwent changes in the 1920s. Hospitals improved their sanitation practices, and more women began to feel confident about delivering their babies there instead of at home, where they had traditionally given birth. Kyvig also details the changes in the educational system, including a growing number of high school graduates and increased college enrollment.

David E. Kyvig teaches history at Northern Illinois University in DeKalb. His research interests include prohibition and constitutional development in the United States during the twentieth century. He is the editor of *Unintended Consequences of Constitutional Amendment.*

A merican family life underwent fundamental alterations in the early twentieth century. Shifts occurred at an earlier time and faster pace in urban areas but gradually spread throughout the nation. Courtship, the process of identifying and engaging a life partner, changed most dramatically, but other aspects of family life, ranging from childbearing to marital expectations and responses when they were not fulfilled, evolved as well.

As recently as the first decade of the century, much courtship had taken place in the home according to well-defined customs.

David E. Kyvig, *Daily Life in the United States, 1920–1939: Decades of Promise and Pain.* Westport, CT: Greenwood Press, 2002. Copyright © 2002 by David E. Kyvig. All rights reserved. Reproduced by permission of the publisher.

A young man would be encouraged to "call" on a young woman. In doing so, he would meet her parents, talk to her in the family parlor, perhaps be offered refreshments, possibly be entertained by her piano playing or singing, and ultimately be encouraged to call again or discouraged from doing so. This social ritual, originating with the upper class, common within the middle class, and copied insofar as possible by families of more modest means, gave eligible women and watchful parents some power over the courtship process. Men could, of course, decline to call, but if they did proceed, they ventured into the woman's environment. If the courtship progressed, the couple might move from the parlor to the still highly visible front porch or attend a public function together, but only well along in the process could a young lady properly consent to the privacy involved in going for a buggy ride alone with her suitor.

"Dating" began to replace calling early in the twentieth century. Homes in the urban environment, in which more and more people found themselves, provided, especially for those of lower income, less space for receiving and entertaining guests. At the same time, cities offered greater possibilities outside the home. Gradually, courting couples began going on dates, prearranged excursions to soda and coffee shops, movie theaters, restaurants, and other places where, even in the midst of a crowd, they experienced less supervision and greater privacy than in the parlor. The automobile further extended the range of possibilities for dating couples, not only as transportation to entertainment but as a place for private intimacy. As the possibilities of a nonmoving automobile began to be appreciated, the term "lover's lane" entered the vocabulary.

Since dates cost money and males were far more likely to be able to earn cash for such purposes, dating tended to give men greater control over courtship. Since they were now the hosts, men gained control over their choice of partner and the entire process; indeed it was considered improper for a woman to propose a date, though she might hint that she would welcome a man's invitation. As costs mounted, so too did the female sense of obligation and the male expectation of appreciation.

In the 1920s, dating became common practice among the nation's youth. It prevailed not only in the cities where it started but in suburbs and smaller communities as well. Young urban men and women who had left school but had not married or acquired a steady companion, found that they could meet at dance halls, speakeasies and bars, skating rinks, and other public places. Only in rural areas and especially in the South where there was little surplus income, access to automobiles, or commercial entertainment did dating fail to develop and older social patterns persist.

Dating soon ceased to be just a search for a mate. It became a primary means for casual social entertainment for adolescents and postadolescents. [Sociologists] Robert and Helen Lynd observed that in Middletown [the fictional name for Muncie, Indiana], frequent dates using the family automobile had become one of the most common sources of tension between teenagers and their parents. At colleges, and also at high schools as the practice spread, dating came to be regarded as a means of demonstrating popularity. The more numerous and varied the dates and the higher the standing of the persons dated, the higher one's status. Thus, continual and diverse dating became an ideal, and often a practice. For many young people, dating served as general recreation and social self-affirmation, not necessarily courtship of a potential life companion.

The shift from calling to dating encouraged greater sexual exploration and intimacy. Long before the rise of the dating system, young people regularly experimented with kissing games. Engaged couples often enjoyed what was coming to be called "heavy petting," and enough people engaged in premarital intercourse that nearly one-in-ten late-nineteenth-century brides went to the altar pregnant. Dating, however, brought with it freer attitudes about sexuality and more freedom to explore them. . . .

Marriage

As courtship evolved and dating exposed many young people to a greater variety of potential partners, the decision to marry was cast in a new light. Marriage had traditionally been regarded as a partnership for economic, educational, and welfare purposes as much as a social relationship. . . .

A new notion emerged, popularized by psychologists, social service professionals, and educators, that a successful marriage was based primarily on affection and companionship. Denver judge Ben Lindsay, in a 1925 book, wrote that "companionate marriage" succeeded because of mutual devotion, sexual attraction, and respect for spousal equality. Pressure from society, church, or state to stay together could not produce a happy marriage in the absence of personal emotional fulfillment, he continued, and in fact could be prove harmful to a couple and any children they might have. Marriage could not be expected to be tension or conflict free, but husbands and wives who were loving companions could communicate and resolve difficulties. Couples unable or unwilling to do so, Lindsay concluded, were better off separating.

Divorce

Some but not all states eased divorce requirements, their legislators saying that marital happiness was more important for couples (and their children) than family economic security (and the risk of adults and children having to be supported by the state). Divorce skyrocketed, increasing from one per eighteen marriages in the 1880s to one per six in the 1920s, but remarriage likewise became common. In 1930, census takers found only slightly more than one percent of adults listing their current status as divorced, far fewer than at one time had been divorced. The figures had grown fractionally since 1920 and would rise minimally further by 1940, but overall the percentage of the population that divorced and did not remarry remained quite low. People were not turning against marriage, as some concerned observers grimly suggested. Instead they had come to desire a happy and fulfilling family life and, if disappointed in an attempt to achieve it, proved increasingly willing and able to start over rather than accept less. Simply put, emotional and sexual satisfaction was replacing economic security as the standard of marital choice and contentment. . . .

Declining Birthrates

While marriage rates remained fairly steady, childbearing continued its longtime decline. During the nineteenth century the average number of children born to American white women had fallen by half, from 7 to 3.5. Between 1900 and 1929, the birthrate dropped by another third. The birthrate decline was greater among middle-class than working-class families, white than nonwhite families, and native-born than immigrant women. The drop reflected decisions to limit family size and practice birth control to do so. The Lynds discovered that in Middletown almost every upper-class couple used some means of contraception, male condoms primarily, though increasingly, female diaphragms. Far fewer working-class couples understood or practiced birth control. One significant result of these deliberate actions was that growing numbers of women completed their childbearing by their early 30s and spent more of their lives in other pursuits. . . .

Leniency Toward Children

Relationships between parents and their children struck observers such as the Lynds as different from those prior to World War I. Change occurred, most notably, though not exclusively, in middle-class families. The shift stemmed from the growth in the 1920s of a school-centered and automobile-liberated youth culture and the decline during the following decade in parental authority linked to the ability to provide economic security. In general strict discipline and harsh punishment became less evident, two-way communication more so. Younger children came to be treated with more open affection, while adolescents were given greater freedom than in earlier decades. As in other eras laden with change and instability, young people often dealt more easily than their parents with new circumstances, and thereby older children in particular gained greater influence within the family. . . .

Health Care

Staying healthy was an ongoing challenge and a daily uncertainty that most Americans addressed with limited knowledge and resources. During the previous half century, scientific discoveries of bacterial transmission of diseases had produced great advances in the treatment of cholera, smallpox, typhoid fever, tuberculosis, and syphilis. Between 1900 and 1930, the first three almost disappeared, tuberculosis fell from second to tenth as a cause of death, and syphilis was brought under control. The limits of this advance in the understanding of contagious diseases became evident, however, as the influenza epidemic of 1918 claimed a death toll that in the United States alone may have exceeded 500,000 (record keeping was far from perfect), primarily in urban areas.

In the aftermath of the flu epidemic, consciousness spread and concern deepened about the need to ward off germs. Cleanliness took higher priority in many Americans' daily lives than ever before. Concern with sanitation, especially in urban areas, led municipalities to initiate or expand regular street cleaning and garbage pickup. Similar concerns became evident within the home. As indoor toilets and consolidated bathrooms became common, especially in middle-class homes, disinfectant cleaning solutions such as Lysol were heavily promoted and widely used. In 1921 the Johnson & Johnson Company developed a sterile bandage held in place by adhesive tape. Marketed for use over small cuts and sores, it was promoted as the "Band Aid.". . .

Overall improvements in their diets . . . contributed a great deal to healthier and longer lives for most Americans. More serious health problems could not be solved so easily. Modern hospital-centered medical care provided by physicians with specialized training was limited, expensive, and generally used only by the wealthy. People who consulted doctors tended to prefer general practitioners who dispensed a wide range of diagnostic and treatment services from their offices or on home visits, usually at modest cost. Between 1920 and 1940, the number of physicians grew about 7 percent, but slipped from 137 to 133 per 100,000 people in a population that was growing three times as fast. It was easier to gain access to a doctor in urban areas. By 1930, 27 percent of the population lived in cities of 100,000 or more, but 44 percent of all doctors practiced there. The concentration of health care facilities and medical expertise in urban centers already well underway would continue.

Childbirth

The most universal circumstance putting health at risk was childbirth. Until 1938 a majority of births took place at home with the mother typically attended by female relatives, friends, neighbors, or a midwife, and, increasingly, a physician. Husbands generally were excluded. By the 1920s, however, urban women, particularly those of middle-class status, turned more often to hospitals to give birth attended by physicians and nurses specializing in obstetrics. Before World War I, hospitals had been widely viewed as unhealthy places, and in fact as recently as 1912, the death rate among children delivered in hospitals was three times that of those born outside of them. Improvements in hospital sanitation and care rapidly altered those conditions and made hospitals the preferred location for childbirth.

Faith in doctors and hospitals rather than traditional practices at the most risk-filled moment for both women and their children reflected a general growth of confidence in medical science. "Slowly but surely," declared *Good Housekeeping* magazine, "childbirth is being lifted out of the realm of darkness into the spotlight of new science." Male physicians encouraged this shift, regarding birth as a dangerous, pathological process best handled in a hospital where forceps, episiotomy, and anesthesia could ease the process. Most expectant mothers, their natural apprehensions reinforced by their doctors, were happy for the drug-reduced awareness of the delivery followed by the rest and service of a hospital stay. They cheerfully surrendered authority over the birthing experience to male strangers and impersonal hospital routines. Only in later decades would women realize that with safety and comfort came loss of control over an important experience in their lives. Most rural women far from hospitals and poor women unable to afford them continued to give birth at home. The change in middle-class childbirth practices, however, played a great role in the dramatic drop in infant mortality from 86 per 1,000 births in 1920 to 65 per 1,000 by 1930 and 47 per 1,000 by 1940.

Doctors Oppose Medical Insurance

If illness or injury struck, the majority of Americans with modest incomes or less during the 1920s and 1930s most often turned to home remedies and accepted considerable suffering. Medical and hospitalization insurance was practically nonexistent. In 1940, the federal census found only 91,000 people out of 132 million with hospitalization coverage and did not even ask about broader medical coverage. The medical profession resisted any suggestion that might impose external supervision or controls. It resisted the Sheppard-Towner Maternity- and Infancy-Protection Act of 1921. When the possibility of national health insurance as a part of the New Deal social welfare program was broached, the American Medical Association convened a special meeting of its house of delegates to denounce the idea. Consequently, medical care and especially a catastropic emergency remained a possibility that every family or unattached individual had to confront by themselves. Professional care was either an unpredictable burden or completely out of reach.

Education

Educating the younger generation was a task that parents and other elders confronted in every era. Once viewed as a family responsibility, by the start of the twentieth century education had come increasingly to be seen as a matter in which the whole society had a stake to insure that young people became capable workers and good citizens. Mandatory school attendance laws intended to insure at least a minimum of literacy among a state's citizens appeared as early as the 1840s in New England. . . .

Nearly one-in-four students in 1920 attended a school in which there was only one teacher. Two hundred thousand such schools were spread across rural America, most notably in the South where racial segregation further reduced the number of students gathered in any one school. Students often had to walk a mile or more to reach these schools. When they arrived, they were greeted by a teacher who had to provide instruction in all subjects at all grade levels. Many of these rural teachers had only a high school education, or less, themselves. The stock of schoolbooks and equipment was equally meager.

The 1920s saw a great movement toward school consolidation. The advent of the school bus made it possible to bring together in a central location students from a wide area. A consolidated school allowed teachers to concentrate on particular subjects or age groups. Busing permitted students to attend classes with others of the same age and ability. With enough students in one place to justify it, high schools in particular could offer a wider range of courses. The school bus became a symbol of significant educational improvement. By the end of the 1920s the number of one-teacher schools had fallen by a quarter and within another decade by almost half. Only Southern schools for African Americans, stifled by segregation and neglect, failed to share in the progress. . . .

Colleges and Universities

The increase in high school graduates together with the growing demand for better-educated teachers helped stimulate a significant rise in college attendance during the 1920s and 1930s. As the percentage of eighteen to twenty-one year olds attending college doubled from 8 to almost 16 percent, the overall enrollment in American colleges and universities grew from 600,000 to 1.5 million. Most of the enrollment growth involved middle-class students attending nonelite public universities in the Midwest and elsewhere. During these decades, two-out-of-three students attended schools that were coeducational and catered to full-time residents. The private universities and colleges more prominent in eastern states, generally smaller to begin with and often restricted to a single sex, grew more slowly. These elite schools regularly excluded or severely limited admission of immigrants, Jews, and African Americans; all but the latter found public institutions, especially urban schools such as the City College of New York, the University of California Los Angeles, and the University of Cincinnati, more hospitable. Also slow growing were the more socially conservative small colleges operated by many religious denominations and the handful of colleges for African Americans.

Women in the Workplace

Gerald Leinwand

One of the most significant changes that emerged in the 1920s was the increased independence of women as many took jobs outside the home. Their increased numbers in the workplace challenged traditional assumptions about women's "proper place." Although more women moved into the public sphere, however, they seldom held positions of power or great responsibility. In the next selection author Gerald Leinwand describes the status of working women near the end of the decade. He notes that women in 1927 held a variety of jobs, including work as trappers, undertakers, lumberwomen, streetcar conductors, stevedores, and taxi drivers. Economic rewards, though limited, gave women the means to participate more fully in the consumer culture. Leinwand points out that "working girls" spent money on cosmetics, hair bobs, and clothing in order to present an attractive appearance on the job and in their social life. Women achieved further independence when they won the right to vote in 1920. However, according to Leinwand, few women participated in politics near the end of the decade, and those who did cast ballots tended to vote as their husbands did. This excerpt is from Leinwand's book *1927: High Tide of the Twenties*.

Gerald Leinwand is president emeritus of Western Oregon University. He served as founding dean of the School of Education at Bernard M. Baruch College of the City University of New York. He is the author of fourteen books, including *The Pageant of World History*.

B y 1927, one in every five wage earners was a woman, making a formidable army of more than 8.5 million working women. Working women could be found in 537 of the 572 occupational categories listed in the census of 1920. Included among such occupations were that of trapper, horse-trader, banker, technician, undertaker, lumberwoman, paperhanger, freight agent, street-car conductor, switchman and flagman, railroad laborer, longshoreman, stevedore, boatman, and deckhand. "Within the space of a single day, one can ride in a taxi driven by a woman, directed by traffic signals designed by a woman, to the office of a woman engineer, there to look out of the window and observe a woman steeplejack at her trade, or contemplate the task of the woman blacksmith whose forge was passed on the way. . . . Ten years ago a woman in Wall Street was an oddity; today women in Wall Street are almost as frequently met as on Fifth Avenue. . . ." [wrote Miriam Simon Leuck]. These examples of women at work demonstrate that some women, at least, were beginning to make inroads into a man's world. Yet, women faced a formidable array of problems in making their way in industrial America. In the competition of the market place, the business field was by no means a level one.

Problems in the Market Place

Professor Lillian H. Locke of Teachers College, Columbia University, complained that it was "practically impossible for a girl to meet her daily needs as to clothing and keep her health up to par on less than $2,000." According to a study made in 1927, more than one-third of self-supporting "girls" lived in residence clubs and earned less than $1,000 a year. About one-fourth of the group studied spent $40 a year on beauty, cosmetics, hair bobs, and perfumes, and one in every five wore a fur coat. Mrs. Henry Moskowitz, vice president of the Association to Promote Proper Housing for Girls, sympathetically observed that "the working girl's . . . job and social life, perhaps her whole future, depend upon her ability to present an attractive appearance and she knows it." But for whom were the working girls dressing? Were they dressing to snare a husband or land and keep a job?

The *Newark Evening News* commented, "Feminists may fulminate, but girls have not changed much in the last few centuries— the ultimate object is the trapping of the male." The *Brooklyn Eagle* was more evenhanded and observed that what women spent on clothing and beauty "belong among outlays or the business of getting a husband, perhaps, and in any case for the business

of getting and keeping a position." That women both out of necessity and desire were seeking to become self-supporting was
slowly becoming evident and grudgingly acknowledged by the
male-dominated world of business.

Women of 1927 were themselves divided on how best to pursue their goals and there was a great deal of ambivalence about
what those goals should be. The veteran battler for woman suffrage Carrie Chapman Catt, in an article for *Current History* in October 1927, identified the goals of the women's movement as follows: "What is the woman movement and what is its aim? It is a
demand for equality of opportunity between the sexes. It means
that when and if a woman is as well qualified as a man to fill a
position, she shall have an equal and unprejudiced chance to secure it. . . . What will bring the revolt to a close? . . . [A]bsolute
equality of opportunity only will satisfy and therefore close the
woman movement." According to this view, the goals of the
movement were to help women escape from the male-imposed
disabilities under which they continued to work. While the expression "breaking through the glass ceiling" had yet to be coined,
clearly Catt was even then determined to break through it.

New Style Feminists

But in 1927 the hard-edged feminism of Carrie Chapman Catt
was being modified by a softer, if no less ambitious feminism of
the "New Style Feminists" who, wrote Dorothy Dunbar Bromley, were "young women in their twenties and thirties . . . the
truly modern ones, those who admit that a full life calls for marriage and children as well as career . . . convinced that they will
be better wives and mothers for the breadth they gain from func-
tioning outside the home."

The New Style Feminist wanted it all—home, husband, children, and family—but was less aggressive in the fight. According to Bromley, the admonitions of the militant feminists to
"Keep your maiden name," "Come out of the kitchen," "Never
darn a sock," were not worth arguing about. Nevertheless, concluded Bromley, the New Style Feminist "knows that it is her
American, her twentieth-century birthright to emerge from a
creature of instinct into a full-fledged individual who is capable
of molding her own life. And in this respect she holds that she

is becoming man's equal." But that equality was a long ways off. If in 1927, slow progress was being made, the disabilities were likewise formidable.

During the 1920s the "emancipated" woman was more myth than reality. The Nineteenth Amendment (1920) had given women the right to vote, but "the Nineteenth Amendment had few immediate consequences for good or evil" [according to scholar William E. Leuchtenberg]. Women continued to vote in smaller numbers than men and, when they voted at all, they voted as their husbands did. While they did not vote as a bloc, they had yet to learn the art and science of exercising political clout. But the success of the feminist movement in gaining the franchise demonstrated that women would begin to use their enfranchisement to secure both political power and economic parity with men. While women were not yet fully engaged in the struggle for equal pay for equal work, the flapper was on the way out and the working girl, who became the career woman, was on the way in.

The Lure of the Automobile

Charles Merz

The 1920s was one of the most exciting decades in the development of transportation in the United States. Rail lines linked the far corners of the nation, and a new era was about to begin in aviation. However, the most dramatic change was the mass production of automobiles. By 1929 nearly 30 million motor vehicles were on the road in the United States. The automobile gave Americans the freedom to leave home and travel about the country. Service stations, eateries, tourist cabins, and garages sprang up along the roadsides to accommodate these new travelers. In the following extract from his book *The Great American Band Wagon*, published in 1928, Charles Merz describes the motor trip he took through the Midwest in 1925. He notes that the filling stations across America have become standardized—each one with identical architecture and services. He also vividly recounts the conversation of two strangers meeting at a station. Merz concludes that it is Americans' pioneering spirit that fuels their desire to rove around the country in automobiles.

Merz worked for the *New York World* as an associate editor in the 1920s. From 1938 to 1961 he served as the editorial page editor of the *New York Times*.

Take your car beyond its accustomed haunts on a journey of exploration. The short stretch of road with its pop-stands, gas-tanks, water-cans, hot dogs, ukeleles, kewpie dolls and chocolate almond bars to which you are accustomed, and of which you think as something local, is the broad and pulsing artery of a nation.

Perhaps you know the road. It begins almost anywhere, at a farmhouse called Ye Willow Inne, climbs a hill and runs off willingly between two rows of brightly painted numbers on its

Charles Merz, *The Great American Band Wagon*. New York: The John Day Company, 1928.

fences, trees and posts. It is the Dixie Highway, or the Lincoln Highway, or the Lackawanna Trail; it is the Yellowstone Trail, or the Yosemite Trail, or the Roosevelt Million Dollar Highway. It is a broad avenue, and with our national talent for organization we have plastered it with good advice. It is impossible to lose one's way and difficult to lose one's life.

Sights Along the Way

Signboards, cross-bars, death's heads, red lights and alarm bells guard the approach to every danger-spot and warn all travellers that locomotives run on railway tracks. The slightest deviation from the straightaway is forecast half a mile ahead. Hills have their lefts and rights. A white streak cuts the road in two, with a keep-to-your-own-side code protecting the ascending sheep from being fouled by the descending goats. There is every safeguard here which engineering can devise, every service which can be performed by free air-tanks and expert tire-changers, every dissuasion which can be brought to bear to keep travellers from self-destruction. This is the highway of a nation.

Over it travels, for many hours of the day, a vast company of motors. Up and down the well-protected hills, over crossroads carefully chalked for left-hand turns and past bits of roadside history done on billboards, the long procession picks its way. America is cruising. It is bumper to bumper, sometimes, for a mile—with no chance of interfering from the side-lines. Inside his gate a farmer pulls his team up short, and counts a string of seven cars before he sees a loophole in the traffic. The pace is steady, seldom-changing, just a little better than the law allows. Only rarely does the caravan slow down. Then horns toot and heads are thrust out nervously to look ahead. . . .

Filling Stations

The rise of the filling station is coincident with the standardization of America. The same successful methods of efficiency and comfort have swept across the country and the filling stations stand as symbols of their progress. Not by so much as three dents in the contour of its battered water-can does one station differ from another. Each is the product of a national art, perfected and unchanging. There is the low shelter with its gabled roof. There is the custodian in khaki trousers with a shirt open at the throat and an evident scorn for anything which lacks eight cylinders. There are the two great pumps outside his door, precisely like all other pumps, at every other station: consistently of the same height, the same diameter, the same cheery shade of red. There is the half circle of cement driveway which makes an arc between these siphons from the road outside. At one end of this cement is painted in white letters, IN. At the other end is painted in white letters, OUT. Not once in years, in this conformist nation, does it occur to any traveller to mutiny at these designations and attempt the OUT end for his IN.

Here is a scene which can be reproduced in any corner of the country: people doing the same thing in the same way in vast numbers for the same purpose. It is not easy in any other place to observe so clearly that certain American customs have developed an uncompromising ritual. A car pulls up. There follows, in regular order, the disagreement between passengers in the front seat and passengers in the rear seat as to the brand of gasoline purchased at the last station, the dispute as to whether this new brand is the same or not the same, the corollary dispute as to whether it does or does not make the slightest difference, the descent from the car to stretch the legs, the salutation to the agent of the station, the setting of the gauge, the turning of the crank, the shaking of the hose for whatever residue remains inside.

Blindfold a man, whisk him around the continent, set him down in an unknown city, and from watching its manners for an hour he might guess its name. But put him down in front of a filling station, any filling station, and not even a sixth sense could tell him whether he was one mile from the Boston Public Library or lost on the Dakota plains.

Strangers Meet

Listen to the conversation of two travellers who have pulled up at the siphons to buy oil. They are strangers: voyagers who have met by chance and will not meet again.

The first is eating a hot dog and waiting for his change. He looks at the customer on his left, and nods. "Heading for Freeport, neighbour?"

"Freeport? Yeh, soon as I get some gas," his neighbour says.

He too is eating a hot dog while his son removes the wrapper from a box of cracker jack. "Road all right?"

"Road's fair. Sand, though."

"Sand, eh?"

"Yeh, lots of sand. But sand don't make any difference to *this* car."

"No? My car neither."

"My car is great on sand."

"Yeh? My car is a bear on sand."

"Hills, too."

"Hills? Say, this car of mine goes up hills like a pig shot out of a barrel. Why, coming up a hill back there a way I passed three cars—"

"I know. Same way with mine. Just have to touch the throttle—"

"And distance! Say, this car is a bird for distance. Never had her out in my life but I got twenty to the gallon."

"Yeh? This car of mine'll just about get that. Nearer twenty-two, I guess. And run? Say, runs like a locomotive. Haven't had the hood up in two years, I guess."

"No? Me neither. This car of mine—Well, good luck and I'll

Automobile sales boomed during the 1920s as manufacturers began building more reasonably priced models.

have a look at that sand of yours. Here's my change."

Clutches grind. Off on the trail they go, one headed east, one headed west. What does it matter that five miles down the road both will have their coats off, bending over smoky motors? This is a modern, mechanistic age, but are men to have no chance to tell each other sagas?

As the first trail-blazers gathered around friendly fires in the wilderness, so men meet now at filling stations on the well-marked road: stopping to buy gas, light pipes, counsel each other as to roads, trade warnings about speed traps and discourse solemnly of mileage, markets, taxes, Prohibition, Congress, [President Calvin] Coolidge, cords and years without a puncture—pausing on the threshold of a new adventure long enough to tell great tales and boast great boasts.

The filling station is a rare spot, in a country of magnificent distances, for the cross-pollination of ideas.

The Roving Spirit of Americans

Over the hills winds the caravan. No other people run around on wheels as we do. No other people live as large a part of their lives in transit as we do. There are motor cars abroad; but not a tenth as many in all Europe. There are touring clubs in France; there are treks from England into Scotland; but with us alone is it suddenly decided after supper to bring the family motor from its shed and take it of an evening for a run which would be thought a day's expedition, anywhere in Europe.

There is constantly in progress in America a migration beside which, from the point of view of numbers, the flight of the chosen people into Egypt was a disturbance of a minor order. A few thousand people crossed the Nile. Millions cross the Mississippi. There are twenty-two million automobiles in the United States. Assume that at any given moment no more than a mere one per cent. of them is on the road. That still means two hundred and twenty thousand cars forever flitting from one filling station to another, with half a million people on their backs. Where are they going, why are they speeding, what do they hope to find?

Impressions? Yes. Impressions of a never-ending road, a thousand farms, grade-crossing signs, back axles, towns passed through at twenty miles an hour.

Thrills? Yes. Thrills of scenery worth stopping for if there were only time, of police on motorcycles masked as fellow-tourists, of gorgeous sunsets well worth watching if the top were down, of getting home, at last, without a crumpled fender,

Trophies? Yes. Trophies to bring back memories of this day of travel: postcards, toy balloons and paper bathing-girls; fresh eggs, fancy radiator caps and sea-shells with an echo.

Yet surely these are poor rewards for so much travel. Surely it is worth no man's while to drive three hundred miles from break of dawn on Sunday just to add another pennant to his string; or to scurry across country for the expressed purpose of viewing the scenery, without stopping anywhere except to change his tires; or to bring back from a point one hundred and eighty-three miles distant an impression of two dozen policemen and seven cities all alike; or to hurry half the day for the apparent purpose of arriving at a point far enough away to make it necessary to turn at once and hurry home again.

No rational explanation can suffice for wandering so purposeless. It is not a matter of reason. It is something in the blood. We are a young nation and the roving spirit is still robust in us. If we cannot rove for the purpose of settling a continent we shall at least rove for the fun of roving, for the pleasure of seeing something, or for the joy of merely having been.

Changing
Values

CHAPTER
2

Chapter Preface

In the 1920s a cultural conflict developed between those Americans who favored liberation from the country's Victorian past and those who lamented what they viewed as the decaying of morals. The older generation vehemently protested the casting aside of values they considered proper, decent, and holy in favor of modernism. The younger generation believed that personal freedom was their right—including the freedom to reject the sexual taboos of the past and to enjoy dancing, drinking, and smoking. "Never in recent generations," wrote social scientist Freda Kirchway, "have human beings so floundered about outside the ropes of social and religious sanctions."

The First World War was the catalyst for the new attitude of young people. The war had exposed American men and women to horrors never before experienced and caused them to question ideas they had previously accepted as truth. Millions of members of the younger generation fought and died in a war that came to be seen as a mistake by many Americans. Many of the surviving members of the war generation became disillusioned with the values of their elders. Writing about the effect of the war, historian Gilman Ostrander notes, "The whole violent disruption of their lives had an enduring effect. On the home front, bands played, lovers said good-bye, women went into war work, and everybody knew that everything was different and that life must be lived by new rules."

The decade produced a restless culture. In the eyes of some, young people went wild. They challenged traditional codes of proper social behavior by throwing raucous parties, drinking illegal liquor, and dancing in a way that the *Catholic Telegraph* of Cincinnati described as "absolutely indecent." Sexual mores, gender roles, and fashions underwent changes. One of the symbols of this 1920s culture was the flapper, a term used to describe the pleasure-seeking young girls of the time. Although only a small segment of society actually fit this image, journalists and the advertising industry used it widely to represent the rebelliousness of the period.

The struggle between the old and the new America manifested

itself in religious controversies between the modern liberals and the religious fundamentalists. As the 1920s began, church attendance was declining. This decline was often ascribed to the breakdown of morals following the strain of World War I and to the growing materialism that accompanied the nation's new prosperity. However, an even more important cause was the impact of scientific thought upon the churches. The modernists believed that religion should take science into consideration. For the fundamentalists, the Bible, not science, was the ultimate source of truth. The battles between these two schools of thought continued throughout the 1920s. At the end of the decade, Harry Emerson Fosdick, a liberal Protestant minister, teacher, and author, summed up the effect of science upon religion:

> The men of faith might claim for their positions ancient traditions, practical usefulness, and spiritual desirability, but one query could prick all such bubbles: Is it scientific? That question has searched religion for contraband goods, stripped it of old superstitions, forced it to change its categories of thought. . . . Science has become the arbiter of this generation's thought, until to call even a prophet and a seer scientific is to cap the climax of praise.

The cultural clashes between the generations and within the church are only two of the many conflicts that unfolded in the 1920s. In addition, people held vigorous debates over alcohol prohibition, race relations, and the role of women in American society—topics which continue to spark great controversy today.

Revolution in Morals and Manners

Frederick Lewis Allen

Social historian Frederick Lewis Allen presents an engaging account of the 1920s in his book *Only Yesterday.* Published just after the decade ended and in the voice of one who lived in the twenties, the book covers a variety of cultural trends and social events. Allen's intent was to write about the changes that affected the daily lives of Americans. In the following excerpt from the book, he focuses on the younger generation's rejection of the values and customs of their parents' generation. Young women no longer wanted to be the "guardians of morality," dressing modestly and refraining from smoking, drinking, and dancing, he writes. Instead, they wanted to be free to wear short skirts and ride in automobiles with their boyfriends. According to Allen, a number of factors made this "revolution in morals and manners" inevitable. The main factor was the state of mind created by World War I. With so many young soldiers having died on the battlefields of Europe, the new generation felt an urgency to live freely and enjoy life now. In addition, young men and women returning from the war front in Europe had experienced a culture with different standards and customs. Many had acquired a new code of behavior that conflicted with traditional restraints and taboos. Allen also notes that Prohibition, the rise of the automobile, and confession and sex magazines contributed to the changing moral standards in the 1920s.

After teaching English at Harvard University, Frederick Lewis Allen worked on the editorial staff of the *Atlantic Monthly.* He was editor in chief of *Harper's Magazine* from 1941 until his death in 1954. His other works include *Since Yesterday* and *The Big Change.*

A first-class revolt against the accepted American order was certainly taking place during those early years of the Post-

Frederick Lewis Allen, *Only Yesterday: An Informal History of the 1920s.* New York: Harper & Row, 1931. Copyright © 1931 by Frederick Lewis Allen. Copyright © 1957 by Harper & Row Publishers, Inc. Copyright © 1959 by Agnes Rogers Allen. All rights reserved. Reproduced by permission of HarperCollins Publishers, Inc.

war Decade, but it was one with which [Russian revolutionary] V.I. Lenin had nothing whatever to do. The shock troops of the rebellion were not alien agitators, but the sons and daughters of well-to-do American families, who knew little about Bolshevism and cared distinctly less, and their defiance was expressed not in obscure radical publications or in soap-box speeches, but right across the family breakfast table into the horrified ears of conservative fathers and mothers. Men and women were still shivering at the Red Menace [communism] when they awoke to the no less alarming Problem of the Younger Generation, and realized that if the Constitution were not in danger, the moral code of the country certainly was.

The Moral Code

This code, as it currently concerned young people, might have been roughly summarized as follows: Women were the guardians of morality; they were made of finer stuff than men and were expected to act accordingly. Young girls must look forward in innocence (tempered perhaps with a modicum of physiological instruction) to a romantic love match which would lead them to the altar and to living-happily-ever-after; and until the "right man" came along they must allow no male to kiss them. It was expected that some men would succumb to the temptations of sex, but only with a special class of outlawed women; girls of respectable families were supposed to have no such temptations. Boys and girls were permitted large freedom to work and play together, with decreasing and well-nigh nominal chaperonage, but only because the code worked so well on the whole that a sort of honor system was supplanting supervision by their elders; it was taken for granted that if they had been well brought up they would never take advantage of this freedom. And although the attitude toward smoking and drinking by girls differed widely in different strata of society and different parts of the country, majority opinion held that it was morally wrong for them to smoke and could hardly imagine them showing the effects of alcohol.

The war had not long been over when cries of alarm from parents, teachers, and moral preceptors began to rend the air. For the boys and girls just growing out of adolescence were making mince-meat of this code.

Changes in Standard Behavior

The dresses that the girls—and for that matter most of the older women—were wearing seemed alarming enough. In July, 1920, a fashion-writer reported in the *New York Times* that "the American woman . . . has lifted her skirts far beyond any modest limitation," which was another way of saying that the hem was now all of nine inches above the ground. It was freely predicted that skirts would come down again in the winter of 1920–21, but instead they climbed a few scandalous inches farther. The flappers wore thin dresses, short-sleeved and occasionally (in the evening) sleeveless; some of the wilder young things rolled their stockings below their knees, revealing to the shocked eyes of virtue a fleeting glance of shin-bones and knee-cap; and many of them were visibly using cosmetics. "The intoxication of rouge," earnestly explained Dorothy Speare in *Dancers in the Dark*, "is an insidious vintage known to more girls than mere man can ever believe." Useless for frantic parents to insist that no lady did such things; the answer was that the daughters of ladies were doing it, and even retouching their masterpieces in public. Some of them, furthermore, were abandoning their corsets. "The men won't dance with you if you wear a corset," they were quoted as saying.

The current mode in dancing created still more consternation. Not the romantic violin but the barbaric saxophone now dominated the orchestra, and to its passionate crooning and wailing the fox-trotters moved in what the editor of the Hobart College *Herald* disgustedly called a "syncopated embrace." No longer did even an inch of space separate them; they danced as if glued together, body to body, cheek to cheek. Cried the *Catholic Telegraph* of Cincinnati in righteous indignation, "The music is sensuous, the embracing of partners—the female only half dressed—is absolutely indecent; and the motions—they are such as may not be described, with any respect for propriety, in a family newspaper. Suffice it to say that there are certain houses appropriate for such dances; but those houses have been closed by law."

Supposedly "nice" girls were smoking cigarettes—openly and defiantly, if often rather awkwardly and self-consciously. They were drinking—somewhat less openly but often all too efficaciously. There were stories of daughters of the most exemplary parents getting drunk—"blotto," as their companions cheerfully put it—on the contents of the hip-flasks of the new prohibition régime, and going out joyriding with men at four in the morning. And worst of all, even at well-regulated dances they were said to retire where the eye of the most sharp-sighted chaperon could not follow, and in darkened rooms or in parked cars to engage in the unspeakable practice of petting and necking. . . .

Meanwhile innumerable families were torn with dissension over cigarettes and gin and all-night automobile rides. Fathers and mothers lay awake asking themselves whether their children were not utterly lost; sons and daughters evaded questions, lied miserably and unhappily, or flared up to reply rudely that at least they were not dirty-minded hypocrites, that they saw no harm in what they were doing and proposed to go right on doing it. From those liberal clergymen and teachers who prided themselves on keeping step with all that was new came a chorus of reassurance: these young people were at least franker and more honest than their elders had been; having experimented for themselves, would they not soon find out which standards were outworn and which represented the accumulated moral wisdom of the race? Hearing such hopeful words, many good people took heart again. Perhaps this flareup of youthful passion was a flash in the pan, after all. Perhaps in another year or two the boys and girls would come to their senses and everything would be all right again.

They were wrong, however. For the revolt of the younger generation was only the beginning of a revolution in manners and morals that was already beginning to affect men and women of every age in every part of the country.

Causes of the Revolution

A number of forces were working together and interacting upon one another to make this revolution inevitable.

First of all was the state of mind brought about by the war and its conclusion. A whole generation had been infected by the eat-drink-and-be-merry-for-tomorrow-we-die spirit which accompanied the departure of the soldiers to the training camps and the fighting front. There had been an epidemic not only of abrupt war marriages, but of less conventional liaisons. In France, two million men had found themselves very close to filth and annihilation and very far from the American moral code and its defenders; prostitution had followed the flag and willing mademoiselles from Armentières [referring to a popular World War I song] had been plentiful; American girls sent over as nurses and war workers had come under the influence of continental manners and standards without being subject to the rigid protections thrown about their continental sisters of the respectable classes; and there had been a very widespread and very natural breakdown of traditional restraints and reticences and taboos. It was impossible for this generation to return unchanged when the ordeal was over. Some of them had acquired under the pressure of war-time conditions a new code which seemed to them quite defensible; millions of them had been provided with an emotional stimulant from which it was not easy to taper off. Their torn nerves craved the anodynes of speed, excitement, and passion. They found themselves expected to settle down into the humdrum routine of American life as if nothing had happened, to accept the moral dicta of elders who seemed to them still to be living in a Pollyanna land of rosy ideals which the war had killed for them. They couldn't do it, and they very disrespectfully said so. . . .

The Growing Independence of Women

The revolution was accelerated also by the growing independence of the American woman. She won the suffrage in 1920. She seemed, it is true, to be very little interested in it once she had it; she voted, but mostly as the unregenerate men about her did, despite the efforts of women's clubs and the League of Women Voters to awaken her to womanhood's civic opportunity; feminine candidates for office were few, and some of them—such as Governor Ma Ferguson of Texas—scarcely seemed to represent the starry-eyed spiritual influence which, it had been promised, would presently ennoble public life. Few of the younger women could rouse themselves to even a passing interest in politics: to them it was a sordid and futile business, without flavor and without hope. Nevertheless, the winning of the suffrage had its effect. It consolidated woman's position as man's equal.

Even more marked was the effect of woman's growing independence of the drudgeries of housekeeping. Smaller houses were being built, and they were easier to look after. Families were moving into apartments, and these made even less claim upon the housekeeper's time and energy. Women were learning how to make lighter work of the preparation of meals. Sales of canned foods were growing, the number of delicatessen stores had increased three times as fast as the population during the decade 1910–20, the output of bakeries increased by 60 per cent during the decade 1914–24. Much of what had once been housework was now either moving out of the home entirely or being simplified by machinery. The use of commercial laundries, for instance, increased by 57 per cent between 1914 and 1924. Electric washing-machines and electric irons were coming to the aid of those who still did their washing at home; the manager of the local electric power company at "Middletown," a typical small American city, estimated in 1924 that nearly 90 per cent of the homes in the city already had electric irons. The housewife was learning to telephone her shopping orders, to get her clothes ready-made and spare herself the rigors of dress-making, to buy a vacuum cleaner and emulate the lovely carefree girls in the magazine advertisements who banished dust with such delicate fingers. Women were slowly becoming emancipated from routine to "live their own lives.". . .

And as for the unmarried woman, she no longer had to explain why she worked in a shop or an office; it was idleness, nowadays, that had to be defended.

With the job—or at least the sense that the job was a possibility—came a feeling of comparative economic independence. With the feeling of economic independence came a slackening of husbandly and parental authority. Maiden aunts and unmarried daughters were leaving the shelter of the family roof to install themselves in kitchenette apartments of their own. For city-dwellers the home was steadily becoming less of a shrine, more of a dormitory—a place of casual shelter where one stopped overnight on the way from the restaurant and the movie theater to the office. Yet even the job did not provide the American woman with that complete satisfaction which the management of a mechanized home no longer furnished. She still had energies and emotions to burn; she was ready for the revolution.

Like all revolutions, this one was stimulated by foreign propaganda. It came, however, not from Moscow, but from Vienna. Sigmund Freud had published his first book on psychoanalysis at the end of the nineteenth century, and he and [psychiatrist Carl] Jung had lectured to American psychologists as early as 1909, but it was not until after the war that the Freudian gospel began to circulate to a marked extent among the American lay public. The one great intellectual force which had not suffered disrepute as a result of the war was science; the more-or-less educated public was now absorbing a quantity of popularized information about biology and anthropology which gave a general impression that men and women were merely animals of a rather intricate variety, and that moral codes had no universal validity and were often based on curious superstitions. A fertile ground was ready for the seeds of Freudianism, and presently one began to hear even from the lips of flappers that "science taught" new and disturbing things about sex. Sex, it appeared, was the central and pervasive force which moved mankind. Almost every human motive was attributable to it: if you were patriotic or liked the violin, you were in the grip of sex—in a sublimated form. The first requirement of mental health was to have an uninhibited sex life. If you would be well and happy, you must obey your libido. Such was the Freudian gospel as it imbedded itself in the American mind after being filtered through the successive minds of interpreters and popularizers and guileless readers and people who had heard guileless readers talk about it. New words and phrases began to be bandied about the cocktail-tray and the Mah Jong table—inferiority complex, sadism, masochism, Œdipus complex. Intellectual ladies went to Europe to be analyzed; analysts plied new trade in American cities, conscientiously transferring the affections of their fair patients to themselves; and clergymen who preached about the virtue of self-control were reminded by outspoken critics that self-control was out-of-date and really dangerous.

The principal remaining forces which accelerated the revolution in manners and morals were all 100 per cent American. . . .

Each of these diverse influences—the post-war disillusion, the new status of women, the Freudian gospel, the automobile, prohibition, the sex and confession magazines, and the movies—had its part in bringing about the revolution. Each of them, as an influence, was played upon by all the others; none of them could alone have changed to any great degree the folkways of America; together their force was irresistible.

In Defense of the Younger Generation

John F. Carter Jr.

In the 1920s countless magazine articles were written depict-
ing the extravagance, the corrupt manners and morals, and the
uselessness of the younger generation. In this article published
in the *Atlantic Monthly* in 1920, journalist John F. Carter Jr. de-
fends his generation. Carter points out that the critics have little
understanding of why young people reject the values and customs of their parents' generation. The younger generation confronted the horrors of World War I in their formative years, he
writes, and became disillusioned by the world created by their
elders. As a result, young people have been forced to question
and reject many of the beliefs of the older generation. Carter ac-
knowledges that his generation does enjoy the extravagant life,
including dancing and drinking, but notes that having faced so
much death during the war, it is only natural that they should
want to enjoy pleasure now. Carter also emphasizes that the
younger generation is characterized by its strong intent to solve
political and social problems and its "determination to face the
facts of life, ugly or beautiful." He adds that these traits did not
characterize the older generation. John F. Carter Jr. became
widely known as a political commentator in the New Deal era.

I n the May issue of the *Atlantic Monthly* appeared an article en-
titled 'Polite Society,' by a certain Mr. Grundy, the husband of
a very old friend of my family. In kindly manner he

> Mentioned our virtues, it is true,
> But dwelt upon our vices, too.

'Chivalry and Modesty are dead. Modesty died first,' quoth he, but
expressed the pious hope that all might yet be well if the oldsters
would but be content to 'wait and see.' His article is one of the

John F. Carter Jr., "'These Wild Young People,' by One of Them," *Atlantic Monthly*,
September 1920.

best-tempered and most gentlemanly of this long series of Jeremiads against 'these wild young people.' It is significant that it should be anonymous. In reading it, I could not help but be drawn to Mr. Grundy personally, but was forced to the conclusion that he, like everyone else who is writing about my generation, has very little idea of what he is talking about. I would not offend him for the world, and if I apostrophize him somewhat brutally in the following paragraphs, it is only because I am talking of him generically; also because his self-styled 'cousin' is present.

For Mrs. Katharine Fullerton Gerould has come forward as the latest volunteer prosecuting attorney, in her powerful 'Reflections of a Grundy Cousin,' in the August *Atlantic*. She has little or no patience with us. She disposes of all previous explanations of our degeneration in a series of short paragraphs, then launches into her own explanation: the decay of religion. She treats it as a primary cause, and with considerable effect. But I think she errs in not attempting to analyze the causes for such decay, which would bring her nearer to the ultimate truth. . . .

The Fallible Older Generation

I would like to say a few things about my generation.

In the first place, I would like to observe that the older generation had certainly pretty well ruined this world before passing it on to us. They give us this Thing, knocked to pieces, leaky, red-hot, threatening to blow up; and then they are surprised that we don't accept it with the same attitude of pretty, decorous enthusiasm with which they received it, 'way back in the eighteen-nineties, nicely painted, smoothly running, practically fool-proof. 'So simple that a child can run it!' But the child couldn't steer it. He hit every possible telegraph-pole, some of them twice, and ended with a head-on collision for which *we* shall have to pay the fines and damages. Now, with loving pride, they turn over their wreck to us; and, since we are not properly overwhelmed with loving gratitude, shake their heads and sigh, 'Dear! dear! We were so much better-mannered than these wild young people. But then we had the advantages of a good, strict, old-fashioned bringing-up!' How intensely *human* these oldsters are, after all, and how fallible! How they always blame us for not following precisely in their eminently correct Footsteps!

Differing World Outlook

Then again there is the matter of outlook. When these sentimental old worldwreckers were young, the world was such a different place—at least, so I gather from [author] H.G. Wells's picture of the nineties, in *Joan and Peter*. Life for them was bright and pleasant. Like all normal youngsters, they had their little tin-pot ideals, their sweet little visions, their naïve enthusiasms, their nice little sets of beliefs. Christianity had emerged from the blow dealt by [evolution theorist Charles] Darwin, emerged rather in the shape of social dogma. Man was a noble and perfectible creature. Women were angels (whom they smugly sweated in their industries and prostituted in their slums). Right was downing might. The nobility and the divine mission of the race were factors that led our fathers to work wholeheartedly for a millennium, which they caught a glimpse of just around the turn of the century. Why, there were Hague Tribunals! International peace was at last assured, and according to current reports, never officially denied, the American delegates held out for the use of poison gas in warfare, just as the men of that generation were later to ruin [President Woodrow] Wilson's great ideal of a league of nations, on the ground that such a scheme was an invasion of American rights. But still, everything, masked by ingrained hypocrisy and prudishness, seemed simple, beautiful, inevitable.

Forced to Become Realists

Now my generation is disillusionized, and, I think, to a certain extent, brutalized, by the cataclysm which *their* complacent folly engendered. The acceleration of life for us has been so great that into the last few years have been crowded the experiences and the ideas of a normal lifetime. We have in our unregenerate youth learned the practicality and the cynicism that is safe only in unregenerate old age. We have been forced to become realists overnight, instead of idealists, as was our birthright. We have seen man at his lowest, woman at her lightest, in the terrible moral chaos of Europe. We have been forced to question, and in many cases to discard, the religion of our fathers. We have seen hideous peculation, greed, anger, hatred, malice, and all uncharitableness, unmasked and rampant and unashamed. We have been forced to live in an atmosphere of 'to-morrow we die,' and so, naturally, we drank and were merry. We have seen the rottenness and shortcomings of all governments, even the best and most stable. We have seen entire social systems overthrown, and our own called in question. In short, we have seen the inherent beastliness of the human race revealed in an infernal apocalypse.

It is the older generation who forced us to see all this, which has left us with social and political institutions staggering blind in the fierce white light that, for us, should beat only about the enthroned ideal. And now, through the soft-headed folly of these painfully shocked Grundys, we have that devastating wisdom which is safe only for the burned-out embers of grizzled, cautious old men. We may be fire, but it was they who made us play with gunpowder. And now they are surprised that a great many of us, because they have taken away our apple-cheeked ideals, are seriously considering whether or no *their* game be worth *our* candle.

Determined to Face Challenges

But, in justice to my generation, I think that I must admit that most of us have realized that, whether or no it be worth while, we must all play the game, as long as we are in it. And I think that much of the hectic quality of our life is due to that fact and to that alone. We are faced with staggering problems and are forced to solve them, while the previous incumbents are permitted a graceful and untroubled death. All my friends are working and working hard. Most of the girls I know are working. In one way or another, often unconsciously, the great burden put upon us is being borne, and borne gallantly, by that immodest, unchivalrous set of ne'er-do-wells, so delightfully portrayed by Mr. Grundy and the amazing young [novelist F. Scott] Fitzgerald. A keen interest in political and social problems, and a determination to face the facts of life, ugly or beautiful, characterizes us, as it certainly did not characterize our fathers. We won't shut our eyes to the truths we have learned. We have faced so many unpleasant things already,—and faced them pretty well,—that it is natural that we should keep it up.

Now I think that this is the aspect of our generation that annoys the uncritical and deceives the unsuspecting oldsters who are now met in judgment upon us: our devastating and brutal frankness. And this is the quality in which we really differ from

Prohibition and the younger generation's rebellious attitude led to a new moral standard during the 1920s. Here, a flapper shows off her ankle flask of illegal liquor.

our predecessors. We are frank with each other, frank, or pretty nearly so, with our elders, frank in the way we feel toward life and this badly damaged world. It may be a disquieting and misleading habit, but is it a bad one? We find some few things in the world that we like, and a whole lot that we don't, and we are not afraid to say so or to give our reasons. In earlier generations this was not the case. . . .

The trouble with them is that they can't seem to realize that we are busy, that what pleasure we snatch must be incidental and feverishly hurried. We have to make the most of our time.

We actually haven't got so much time for the noble procrastinations of modesty or for the elaborate rigmarole of chivalry, and little patience for the lovely formulas of an ineffective faith. Let them die for a while! They did not seem to serve the world too well in its black hour. If they are inherently good they will come back, vital and untarnished. But just now we have a lot of work, 'old time is still a-flying,' and we must gather rose-buds while we may.

Oh! I know that we are a pretty bad lot, but has not that been true of every preceding generation? At least we have the courage to act accordingly. Our music is distinctly barbaric, our girls are distinctly *not* a mixture of arbutus and barbed-wire. We drink when we can and what we can, we gamble, we are extravagant—but we work, and that's about all that we can be expected to do; for, after all, we have just discovered that we are all still very near to the Stone Age.

We're men and women, long before time, in the flower of our blooded youth. We have brought back into civil life some of the recklessness and ability that we were taught by war. We are also quite fatalistic in our outlook on the tepid perils of tame living. All may yet crash to the ground for aught that we can do about it. Terrible mistakes will be made, but *we* shall at least make them intelligently and insist, if we are to receive the strictures of the future, on doing pretty much as we choose now.

Oh! I suppose that it's too bad that we aren't humble, starry-eyed, shy, respectful innocents, standing reverently at their side for instructions, playing pretty little games, in which they no longer believe, except for us. But we aren't, and the best thing the oldsters can do about it is to go into their respective back-yards and dig for worms, great big pink ones—for the Grundy tribe are now just about as important as they are, and they will doubtless make company more congenial and docile than 'these wild young people,' the men and women of my generation.

A Jazz-Age Flapper

Ellen Welles Page

Flappers were young women of the Jazz Age, or Roaring Twenties, who embodied the exuberance and rebelliousness of youth. They broke away from the preceding generations of women who held to the Victorian image of womanhood. In contrast to the corseted, coiffed, and covered Gibson Girls (sketches of ideal young American women of the 1890s) of twenty years earlier, flappers looked boyish. They abandoned the corset, bobbed their hair, wore rouge and lipstick, and shortened their skirts. This style of dress represented their independence. These innovations and freer socializing with men shocked the older generation. A flapper, Ellen Welles Page, wrote the following excerpt in 1922. In this open letter to parents, she implores adults to be more understanding of the struggles of young people in the postwar era. She also asks that parents help the younger generation by giving them confidence and understanding when they make mistakes. She points out that it is up to the parents "who have supervision of us of less ripe experience to guide us sympathetically."

If one judge by appearances, I suppose I am a flapper. I am within the age limit. I wear bobbed hair, the badge of flapperhood. (And, oh, what a comfort it is!), I powder my nose. I wear fringed skirts and bright-colored sweaters, and scarfs, and waists with Peter Pan collars, and low-heeled "finale hopper" shoes. I adore to dance. I spend a large amount of time in automobiles. I attend hops, and proms, and ball-games, and crew races, and other affairs at men's colleges. But none the less some of the most thoroughbred superflappers might blush to claim sistership or even remote relationship with such as I. I don't use rouge, or lipstick, or pluck my eyebrows. I don't smoke (I've tried it, and don't like it), or drink, or tell "peppy stories." I don't pet. And, most unpardonable infringement of all the rules and regulations of Flapperdom, I haven't a line! But then—there are many degrees of flapper. There is the semi-flapper; the flapper; the super-

Ellen Welles Page, "A Flapper's Appeal to Parents," *Outlook*, December 6, 1922.

flapper. Each of these three main general divisions has its degrees of variation. I might possibly be placed somewhere in the middle of the first class.

I think every one realizes by this time that there has been a marked change in our much-discussed tactics. Jazz has been modified, and probably will continue to be until it has become obsolete. Petting is gradually growing out of fashion through being overworked. Yes, undoubtedly our hopeless condition is improving. But it was not for discussing these aspects of the case that began this article.

I want to beg all you parents, and grandparents, and friends, and teachers, and preachers—you who constitute the "older generation"—to overlook our shortcomings, at least for the present, and to appreciate our virtues. I wonder if it ever occurred to any of you that it required brains to become and remain a successful flapper? Indeed it does! It requires an enormous amount of cleverness and energy to keep going at the proper pace. It requires self-knowledge and self-analysis. We must know our capabilities and limitations. We must be constantly on the alert. Attainment of flapperhood is a big and serious undertaking!

"Brains?" you repeat, skeptically. "Then why aren't they used to better advantage?" That is exactly it! And do you know who is largely responsible for all this energy's being spent in the wrong directions? You! You parents, and grandparents, and friends, and teachers, and preachers—all of you! "The war!" you cry. "It is the effect of the war!" And then you blame prohibition. Yes! Yet it is you who set the example there! But this is my point: Instead of helping us work out our problems with constructive, sympathetic thinking and acting, you have muddled them for us more hopelessly with destructive public condemnation and denunciation.

A Plea for Patience and Understanding

Think back to the time when you were struggling through the teens. Remember how spontaneous and deep were the joys, how serious and penetrating the sorrows. Most of us, under the present system of modern education, are further advanced and more thoroughly developed mentally, physically, and vocationally than were our parents at our age. We hold the infinite possibilities of the myriads of new inventions within our grasp. We have learned to take for granted conveniences, and many luxuries, which not so many years ago were as yet undreamed of. We are in touch with the whole universe. We have a tremendous problem on our hands. You must help us. Give us confidence—not distrust. Give us practical aid and advice—not criticism. Praise us when praise is merited. Be patient and understanding when we make mistakes.

We are the Younger Generation. The war tore away our spiritual foundations and challenged our faith. We are struggling to regain our equilibrium. The times have made us older and more experienced than you were at our age. It must be so with each succeeding generation if it is to keep pace with the rapidly advancing and mighty tide of civilization. Help us to put our knowledge to the best advantage. Work with us! That is the way! Outlets for this surplus knowledge and energy must be opened. Give us a helping hand.

Youth has many disillusionments. Spiritual forces begin to be felt. The emotions are frequently in a state of upheaval, struggling with one another for supremacy. And Youth does not understand. There is no one to turn to—no one but the rest of Youth, which is as perplexed and troubled with its problems as ourselves. Everywhere we read and hear the criticism and distrust of older people toward us. It forms an insurmountable barrier between us. How can we turn to them?

"Parents, Study Your Children"

In every person there is a desire, an innate longing, toward some special goal or achievement. Each of us has his place to fill. Each of us has his talent—be it ever so humble. And our hidden longing is usually for that for which nature equipped us. Any one will do best and be happiest doing that which he really likes and for which he is fitted. In this "age of specialists," as it has been called, there is less excuse than ever for persons being shoved into niches in which they do not belong and cannot be made to fit. The lives of such people are great tragedies. That is why it is up to you who have the supervision of us of less ripe experience to guide us sympathetically, and to help us find, encourage, and develop our special abilities and talents. Study us. Make us realize that you respect us as fellow human beings, that you have confidence in us, and, above all, that you expect us to live up to the highest ideals, and to the best that is in us.

It must begin with individuals. Parents, study your children. Talk to them more intimately. Respect their right to a point of view. Be so understanding and sympathetic that they will turn to you naturally and trustfully with their glowing joys or with their heartaches and tragedies. Youth has many of the latter because Youth takes itself so seriously. And so often the wounds go unconfessed, and, instead of gradually healing, become more and more gnawing through suppression until of necessity relief is sought in some way which is not always for the best. . . .

Serve as an Inspiration to Us

Oh, parents, parents everywhere, point out to us the ideals of truly glorious and upright living! Believe in us, that we may learn to believe in ourselves, in humanity, in God! Be the living examples of your teachings, that you may inspire us with hope and courage, understanding and truth, love and faith. Remember that we are the parents of the future. Help us to be worthy of the sacred trust that will be ours. Make your lives such an inspiration to us that we in our turn will strive to become an inspiration to our children and to the ages! Is it too much to ask?

Religious Fundamentalism

W.B. Riley

Fundamentalism was a movement begun by Christian evan-
gelical conservatives in the late nineteenth century. Fundamentalists believed that the Bible is historically accurate and infalli-
ble. They rejected modernist theologians who attempted to
integrate new findings in science and history into their understanding of Christianity. Fundamentalists also opposed the teaching of evolution, which contradicted their understanding of bib-
lical scriptures. In the 1920s W.B. Riley, a Minneapolis minister
and evangelist, wrote books, established Bible institutes, and set
up local associations around the country to challenge the views
of modernists. In the next selection, written in 1927, Riley out-
lines the major doctrines of fundamentalists, including the belief
that the Bible represents the direct word of God and is therefore
"the supreme and final authority in faith and life." Riley also argues against modernist theologians who reject some passages of
the Bible as untrue or incorrect and who offer new interpreta-
tions of other passages. Such arbitrary judgments by man, he as-
serts, make the teachings of the Bible absurd and meaningless.
W.B. Riley was a pastor of the First Baptist Church of Minneapolis, a founder of the Anti-Evolution League, and the president of
the World's Christian Fundamentals Association.

W hat is Fundamentalism? It would be quite impossible,
within the limits of a single article, so to treat the subject
as to satisfy all interested parties. There are too many features of
this Christian faith for one to attempt a delineation. But there
are at least three major propositions that must appear in any adequate reply, and they are these: It is the Christian Creed; it is
the Christian Character; it is the Christian Commission.

W.B. Riley, "The Faith of the Fundamentalists," *Current History*, vol. XXVI, June 1927.

The Greater Christian Doctrines

Fundamentalism undertakes to reaffirm the greater Christian doctrines. Mark this phrase, "the greater Christian doctrines." It does not attempt to set forth every Christian doctrine. It has never known the elaboration that characterizes the great denominational confessions. But it did lay them side by side, and, out of their extensive statements, elect nine points upon which to rest its claims to Christian attention. They were and are as follows:

1. We believe in the Scriptures of the Old and New Testaments as verbally inspired by God, and inerrant in the original writings, and that they are of supreme and final authority in faith and life.

2. We believe in one God, eternally existing in three persons, Father, Son and Holy Spirit.

3. We believe that Jesus Christ was begotten by the Holy Spirit, and born of the Virgin Mary, and is true God and true man.

4. We believe that man was created in the image of God, that he sinned and thereby incurred not only physical death, but also that spiritual death which is separation from God; and that all human beings are born with a sinful nature, and, in the case of those who reach moral responsibility, become sinners in thought, word and deed.

5. We believe that the Lord Jesus Christ died for our sins according to the Scriptures as a representative and substitutionary sacrifice; and that all that believe in Him are justified on the ground of His shed blood.

6. We believe in the resurrection of the crucified body of our Lord, in His ascension into Heaven, and in His present life there for us, as High Priest and Advocate.

7. We believe in "that blessed hope," the personal, premillennial and imminent return of our Lord and Saviour, Jesus Christ.

8. We believe that all who receive by faith the Lord Jesus Christ are born again of the Holy Spirit and thereby become children of God.

9. We believe in the bodily resurrection of the just and the unjust, the everlasting felicity of the saved and the everlasting conscious suffering of the lost.

It would seem absolutely clear, therefore, that many of the liberal writers of recent years have never taken the pains to ask for the basis of our belief. . . .

Modernism when it comes to deal with the Fundamentals movement is suddenly possessed with a strange imagination. If you want to know what the movement is *not* and who its leaders are *not*, read their descriptions of both. Certainly as to what we believe, the above declaration leaves no doubt, and only the man ignorant of the Bible or utterly indifferent to its teachings, could ever call into question that these nine points constitute the greater essentials in the New Testament doctrinal system.

Fundamentalism insists upon the plain intent of Scripture-speech. The members of this movement have no sympathy whatever for that weasel method of sucking the meaning out of words and then presenting the empty shells in an attempt to palm them off as giving the Christian faith a new and another interpretation. The absurdities to which such a spiritualizing method may lead are fully revealed in the writings of Mary Baker Eddy [leader of the Christian Science movement] and modernists in general. When one is permitted to discard established and scientific definitions and to create, at will, his own glossary, language fails to be [any] longer a vehicle of thought, and inspiration itself may mean anything or nothing, according to the preference of its employer. . . .

Fundamentalism is forever the antithesis of modernist critical theology. It is made up of another and an opposing school. Modernism submits all Scripture to the judgment of man. According to its method he may reject any portion of the Book as uninspired, unprofitable, and even undesirable, and accept another portion as from God because its sentences suit him, or its teachings inspire him. Fundamentalism, on the contrary, makes the Bible "the supreme and final authority in faith and life." Its teachings determine every question upon which they have spoken with some degree of fullness, and its mandates are only disregarded by the unbelieving, the materialistic and the immoral. Fundamentalists hold that the world is illumined and the Church is instructed and even science itself is confirmed, when true, and condemned when false, by the clear teachings of the open Book, while Liberalism, as *The Nation* once said, "pretends to preach the higher criticism by interpreting the sacred writings as esoteric fables." In other words, the two have nothing in common save church membership, and all the world wonders that they do or can remain together; and the thinking world knows that but one tie holds them, and that is the billions of dollars invested.

Modernists Have Filched the Universities Created by Fundamentalists

Nine out of ten of those dollars, if not ninety-nine out of every hundred of them, spent to construct the great denominational universities, colleges, schools of second grade, theological seminaries, great denominational mission stations, the multiplied hospitals that bear denominational names, the immense publication societies and the expensive magazines, were given by Fundamentalists and filched by modernists. It took hundreds of years to collect this money and construct these institutions. It has taken only a quarter of a century for the liberal bandits to capture them, and the only fellowship that remains to bind modernists and Fundamentalists in one body, or a score of bodies, is the Irish fellowship of a free fight—Fundamentalists fighting to retain what they have founded, and modernists fighting to keep their hold on what they have filched. It is a spectacle to grieve angels and amuse devils; but we doubt not that even the devils know where justice lies, and the angels from heaven sympathize with the fight and trust that faithful men will carry on.

Creed alone is neither competent nor convincing. Creed, in the abstract, is cold and dead, but creed incarnate constitutes Christianity as positively as the word incarnate constituted the Christ. Christianity roots in a creed and fruits in character. . . .

Creed and Conduct

The man who combines an unshaken faith in the authority and integrity of the Bible with an aggressive uprightness in conduct, is the man who approaches, in some human measure, the perfect copy in the Christ life, for in His words the most watchful enemies were unable to catch Him and against His works no worthy objection was ever urged. . . .

The proofs of Fundamentalism, then, are not in words, but in deeds. This has been the conception of Fundamentalists from the first, for while the World's Christian Fundamentals Association, as an organization, is but nine years old, Christian Fundamentalism has back of it two thousand years of glorious history. It was

Fundamentalism that produced the Book of Acts. You will find every essential feature of our creed in Peter's sermon at Pentecost, even to the Second Coming. It was Fundamentalism that conquered the Roman Empire, and in one hundred years revised the conduct of men and brought in and established laws of righteousness, including regard for the Sabbath, the rights of the Church in the State, and the recognition of law versus anarchy. It was Fundamentalism that challenged corrupt Rome in [sixteenth-century reformer] Martin Luther's time and called out a people whose clean and wholesome conduct became the condemnation of foul papal practices, and turned the thought of the general public from the coercive measures of a corrupt Church to the intelligent and voluntary service of the King of Glory. It was Fundamentalism that faced the heresy of Deism one hundred and forty years ago, and in an open and fair field fought the battle to the finish, and slew that infidel monster as effectually as Saint George was ever imagined to have trampled the dragon. And it was Fundamentalist evangelists who so uniformly led the common people back to the "faith once delivered" as to bury atheism practically out of sight for one hundred years.

But to battling, Fundamentalism has forever added building. Of all the colleges that Congregationalism, of nearly one hundred years ago, contributed to America, commencing with Harvard [University] in the East, dotting practically every State in the Union with at least one, Fundamentalism built the entire line. The same remark applies to the Baptist, Presbyterian and Methodist institutions known to the whole American continent. . . .

Of what value is our boasted accomplishment at mechanical and electrical and chemical discoveries, if, while they are contributing to our material prosperity, they are more rapidly still undermining our morals? The whole doctrine of evolution is not only lacking a single illustration in the processes of nature, but it is being disproven by the program of man, for mechanical invention resulting in moral decay, is not even progress, but degeneration instead. Babylon, Persia, Greece and Rome—each of them reached a climax of material development and then deliberately committed suicide by moral degeneracy.

The Rise of Consumer Culture

Sharon Murphy

Before the 1920s very few people made purchases on credit. The ethos of self-disciplined, self-reliant Americans was not to spend money they had not yet earned. Thrift and delayed gratification were considered virtues. However, in the 1920s merchandisers began to promote "installment plan buying," a method of purchasing a good by putting a certain amount of money down and making monthly payments until the item is paid off. Advertisers of a wide variety of durable goods including cars, washing machines, and toasters began to urge consumers to "buy now, pay later." These advertisements were influential, and Americans began to buy goods on credit rather than waiting until they had saved enough money to pay for them. Many historians believe that this period marks the beginning of the rise of a consumption-oriented society in America. In this selection Sharon Murphy describes the development of installment plan buying and its impact on American values. Murphy is a graduate student and instructor in American history at the University of Virginia.

A fter several decades of urbanization and industrialization, post–World War I America was marked by a rapid increase in the availability of mass-produced commodities. For the growing middle-class population, the twentieth-century American dream had become based on the acquisition and consumption of this rising tide of commodities. Economic historians like Martha Olney have described this period as a consumer durables revolution, characterized by an increase in both the average household expenditure for durable goods and the amount of installment credit issued to help pay for these goods.

A critical precursor to this revolution was a transformation of

Sharon Murphy, "The Advertising of Installment Plans," *Essays in History, Volume 37*. Charlottesville: University of Virginia Press, 1995. Copyright © 1995 by the University of Virginia Press. Reproduced by permission.

the prevailing consumer attitudes towards incurring debt, and particularly a removal of the stigma against buying on installments. The idea of being in debt had always been looked down upon by the American public, yet the expansion of the market for consumer durables depended upon an increase in credit transactions. The birth of the automobile installment finance company in 1919 provided the foundation for this transformation, creating a successful example of installment selling in a major industry.

The catalyst to this change, however, lay not in the mere availability of installment credit but in the selling of the concept of debt through advertising. During the 1920s, businesses increasingly utilized advertising as a method not only to sell their products, but also as a means to convince the American public to buy on installments. Both the quantity and the quality of advertisements which mentioned installment plans rose significantly during this period, particularly in local publications. By 1929, these advertisements reflected the general acceptance of installment buying as a way to finance consumption and demonstrated that this shift in attitudes had reached its completion.

The Origins of Installment Buying

Installment buying is a specific method of purchasing goods on credit, distinct from other forms of credit such as loans or credit cards. Unlike a loan which entails a direct exchange of money from one party to another, these transactions always involve a transfer of wealth in the form of goods or services. A partial payment may be made at the time of the sale but full payment is deferred until some future date. In contrast with credit card purchases, an exact schedule of payments is enumerated at the time of the sale. The remainder owed is paid in specific quantities at successive intervals.

Installment buying most commonly occurs in conjunction with the sale of durable goods. The Department of Commerce defines a durable good as any household product that can be used, on average, for three years or more. Durable goods are often divided by economists into major and minor durables. [According to historian Thomas Juster] major durables are goods "characterized by relatively long service lives, by the existence of commercial markets in which the services of similar assets [can] be purchased, and by unit costs high enough so that purchase with borrowed funds [is] a common method of acquisition." Goods such as automobiles and automobile parts, furniture, household appliances, radios, phonographs, and pianos fall into this category. Minor durables are defined as all other durable goods, such as china and tableware, house furnishings, jewelry, books, maps, and some toys. . . .

Overall, selling on installments was a very limited practice prior to the Civil War. It was confined primarily to goods which could be easily resold and the terms of payment tended to be rather stringent. It was a privilege enjoyed only by those customers with good credit histories and with income levels high enough to ensure the ability to meet the contract terms. As a business method, installment selling proved to be highly profitable for those retailers who chose to utilize it.

At the end of the nineteenth century, however, retailers of lower grade commodities began to extend installment credit to lower income families who were higher credit risks. The practice became commonly used by the poorest families who began to buy the necessities required for everyday living on installments. This was particularly true in cities like New York, where peddlers sold goods on installment to the rising tide of immigrants. Many of these peddlers took advantage of the immigrants by delivering products of much poorer quality, than what was originally selected or by greatly overvaluing the goods. Although the idea of being in debt had always been looked down upon, it was at this time that the negative reputation of installment buying was intensified. No longer a privilege reserved for the upper classes, it became "symbolic of poverty, prodigality, [and] gullibility" [according to credit expert Rolf Nugent].

The Success of Automobile Installment Plans

This was still the prevailing attitude towards installment buying in 1919 when General Motors created the General Motors Acceptance Corporation (GMAC), the first automobile installment finance company. This organization was originally developed in response to the large seasonal fluctuations which automobile sales experienced. Before closed cars became popular, automobile sales occurred primarily in the spring and summer. There were several months when assembly lines ran at full capacity, and then long periods when they were practically dormant and large numbers of workers had to be laid off. The car manufacturers wanted to remedy this problem by building up inventories during the slower months and then selling them off during the peak season. They expected this surplus to be stored by the individual dealers, but these dealers lacked the capital necessary to fund this storage. The solution to this problem came with the development of the sales finance company which provided the capital essential to maintain these inventories.

Eventually, these companies expanded into automobile installment finance companies for middle- and lower-middle-class consumers. Without credit, a customer needed to save enough cash to cover the full price of the car. That was impossible for most Americans. As Olney noted, in order to purchase an automobile with cash during this time period, a typical American family would have to save for almost five years. With the spread of credit between 1919 and 1929, the percentage of households buying cars on installment more than tripled, rising from 4.9% to 15.2%. The creation of GMAC accounted for a large portion of this increase. In 1925, GMAC was three times larger than its nearest competitor, financing almost half of all installment purchases of automobiles that took place in that year.

With this dramatic increase in the installment selling of automobiles came the expansion of this technique into the markets for other major durable goods. According to credit expert Rolf Nugent, the success of automobile installment plans "tended to remove the stigma which installment selling had acquired at the hands of low-grade installment merchants in the 1890s." In fact, credit was used in the purchases of up to 90% of major durable goods by the end of the 1920s. Average purchases of major durable goods rose from 3.7% of disposable income between 1898 and 1916 to 7.2% between 1922 and 1929. Accompanying this rise in purchases of durables was a drop in the personal savings rate, from 6.4% of disposable income in the former period to 3.8% in the latter.

This rise in installment purchases of major durable goods was contingent on a fundamental transformation of consumer attitudes towards incurring debt. In a report commissioned in 1926 by the American Bankers Association, economist Milan Ayres commented, "During the nineteenth century the things that a self-respecting, thrifty American family would buy on the installment plan were a piano, a sewing machine, some expensive articles of furniture, and perhaps a set of books. People who made such purchases didn't talk about them. Installment buying wasn't considered quite respectable." The change in the popular attitude towards installment buying which primarily occurred between the years 1922 and 1929 was therefore imperative to this revolution in consumer durables. . . .

The number of advertisements which mentioned installment plans did not really begin to increase until about 1922. Although GMAC had been created in 1919, the change in the popular perception of installment buying was initially very gradual since many customers still remained wary of making purchases on credit. By 1922, however, the overwhelming success of installment buying in the automobile industry began to attract manufacturers and dealers of other major durable goods. A boost was given to installment sales of furniture, pianos and sewing machines, but a major portion of the increase in installment selling can be traced to new products just entering the market or older products which had previously avoided offering installment plans. These goods included phonographs, washing machines, electric refrigerators, vacuum cleaners, and radio sets. This rise in installment sales was reflected in the steady increase in advertisements which mentioned the availability of installment plans, especially after 1922. . . .

There were several ways in which advertisements during the 1920s tried to sell the idea of installment buying to the American public. One way was to appeal to the traditional sentiments that had originally made installment buying unattractive. An advertisement in 1920 [in the *Richmond Times-Dispatch*] for a New Edison phonograph called its budget plan "a real thrift idea. It helps you purchase your New Edison without paying spot cash and without increasing your monthly allowance for enjoyment." A similar advertisement for Pettit and Company furniture stores stated, "Buying home furnishings on credit at Pettit's is a thrifty habit. The easy weekly installments are like savings put in the bank, that pay big dividends in happiness and service." Thus, these advertisements tried to show that there was no contradiction between incurring debt and the time-honored American virtue of thrift.

Advertisers also endeavored to elevate the reputation of installment buying in other ways. Several businesses used the adjective "dignified" to describe their installment plans and one furniture company even called itself "The House of Dignified Credit." Other advertisements went even further by attempting to convince the purchasers that they would actually save money by buying on installments. Bloomberg-Michael Furniture Company said that its "plan enables you to save at least 25% in your purchase and gives you the benefit of extended time." This advertisement did not, however, explain exactly how installment buying would save the consumer money.

A Rising Consumption Ethic

Equating installment buying with thrifty ideals softened popular fears of the practice. By incorporating the traditional economic values of the average, middle-class American into their descriptions of installment plans, advertisers depicted installment buying as a practice which aided consumers in their attempts to make frugal purchases. Paying in installments was characterized as the modern equivalent of saving money in the bank. By placing installment buying in a traditional context, advertisers helped consumers adjust to the notion of paying a small down payment with the remainder to be paid in easy weekly or monthly installments. . . .

Advertisers also emphasized the convenience of buying on time. As many advertisements explained, the consumer could use the product while it was still being paid for, rather than having to save over several years and being deprived of current enjoyment. These advertisements introduced and played on new ideas of leisure and pleasure. They encouraged customers to "ride as you pay" or "play as you pay." For just "a small amount down" you could "get want you want now." Rather than waiting to buy a new refrigerator or baby carriage, retailers "are making it easy to get these things, right now when you need them" [according to an ad in the *Richmond Times-Dispatch*]. These advertisements played upon the rising consumption ethic by which Americans increasingly desired to buy goods immediately rather than postponing their purchases until enough money had accumulated in the bank. Customers were told that they should not wait to obtain the commodities they desired, nor did they have to wait any longer. The availability of installment plans made it possible for them to fulfill these desires almost instantly. . . .

"Nearly Everyone" Prefers to Pay Later

By the end of the decade, the wholly positive portrayals of installment plans reflected the complete transformation in consumer attitudes. Words like "convenient," "low-cost," and "easy" continued to be used in the descriptions of payment plans. Additionally, the image of joyful dealers who "welcome business on the General Motors deferred payment plan" [the words of an ad in the April 1929 issue of *Good Housekeeping*] was still a common sight. Advertisements of this time period went one step further, however, demonstrating that buying on installments had become a permanent aspect of the twentieth-century American dream.

One of the most telling examples of an advertisement which fully reflected the completion of this transformation in consumer attitudes was a LaSalle automobile advertisement from a 1928 issue of *Good Housekeeping*. In mentioning the available installment plan it poignantly stated, "If you prefer to buy out of income, as nearly everyone does today, the General Motors plan is very liberal." At this point, the journey from a world in which customers were expected to pay with cash and were discouraged from buying on installments, to a world in which salesmen actually encouraged the use of installment plans was complete. Customers who made purchases on installments were no longer depicted as a minority group deviating from the normal course of action. It was now the people who insisted on paying in cash who seemed overly traditional and backward looking. As historian Frederick Lewis Allen commented in 1931, "People were getting to consider it old-fashioned to limit their purchases to the amount of their cash balances."

By the end of the 1920s, installment plans had become the primary way for a middle-class family to attain a piece of the American dream. People who had formerly shied away from acquiring debt now accepted installment buying as a means to finance modern consumption. This transformation in consumer attitudes resulted from a gradual change in the depiction of installment buying in advertisements. Retailers increasingly utilized this medium in order to convince consumers to buy on installments, both influencing and reflecting popular perceptions of this practice. By the eve of the Great Depression, they had intimately linked installment buying to the attainment of the American dream.

Arts and Entertainment

CHAPTER 3

Chapter Preface

Technological advances and growing industries in the 1920s assured the majority of Americans higher wages and increased leisure time to pursue both new and old forms of entertainment and art, including spectator sports, movies, and literature. People all around the country indulged in these pastimes, contributing to the ongoing development of a national culture.

In search of excitement, Americans congregated like never before at baseball diamonds, football stadiums, and ringside seats, as sports became a national mania. Radio brought professional sports into people's homes, boosting the fame of sports heroes. One of the many sports heroes of the decade was baseball player George Herman Ruth—the amazing Babe Ruth. Boxer Jack Dempsey was another of America's first great sports heroes. His savage style captivated the public in the 1920s and made him as popular a figure as Babe Ruth. Journalist H.L. Mencken wrote: "Dempsey has a wallop in his right hand like the collision of a meteorite with the Alps." Women also became sports stars for the first time. In 1926 New Yorker Gertrude F. Ederle became the first woman to swim the English Channel. "People said women couldn't swim the Channel but I proved they could," Ederle remarked.

In the 1920s Hollywood stars joined sports heroes in the ranks of the nation's idols. Movie actors such as Rudolph Valentino, Clara Bow, Mary Pickford, Douglas Fairbanks, and Charlie Chaplin delighted the millions of viewers who went to movies in the cities and even in rural areas. The popularity of the movies soared as films increasingly featured glamour, sophistication, and sex appeal.

The arts thrived in the stimulating environment of the twenties. Prior to this time, American arts had reflected European influences. As American writers, painters, musicians, and architects interpreted the modern world, a distinctive American identity emerged. For example, F. Scott Fitzgerald arrived on the literary scene in the twenties. According to author Christine N. Perkins, Fitzgerald "best typifies the ethos of the flamboyant upper class in the prosperous 1920s." His novels gave voice to the confusion of the decade and brought to life the party atmosphere of the time.

His novel *The Great Gatsby*, published in 1925, is widely considered to be his best work. Many other talented writers emerged in the 1920s, including the fresh new voice of Ernest Hemingway. After serving as an ambulance driver in France during World War I, Hemingway spent time in Paris writing short stories, poems, and novels. His first novel, *The Sun Also Rises* (1926), is a story of young, expatriate Americans living in Europe.

African Americans were also making many contributions to the literary world of the 1920s. One of the most famous poets of the time was Langston Hughes, who became one of the leaders of the cultural movement known as the Harlem Renaissance. This movement afforded opportunities for African Americans to express themselves in writing, art, and music. The literary works of Claude McKay and Jean Toomer show how African Americans lived—their joys, their sorrows, and their daily struggles in a segregated society. The Harlem Renaissance had a lasting impact on American culture, as African Americans developed a sense of pride in their race and embraced the struggle to expand civil rights.

African American culture also expressed itself through jazz, a new form of improvisational music. Jazz began in New Orleans, quickly spreading across the country and eventually abroad. Jazz greats included Louis Armstrong, Joe Oliver, Duke Ellington, George Gershwin, and Cole Porter. Jazz clubs flourished in the big cities and attracted white audiences as well as African Americans. Though some people rejected jazz, Sergei Koussevitzky, then conductor of the Boston Symphony, correctly predicted that jazz had come to stay.

In the 1920s, for the first time, large numbers of Americans had the leisure time and money to indulge their taste for fun. Also for the first time, technology and the rise of mass production allowed millions of Americans to enjoy the same kinds of pastimes. In the 1920s the United States developed a mass culture that was fed by technologies such as the radio that provided common access to the same information and entertainment. As author Phillip Margulies writes, "Rich and poor, highbrow and lowbrow, country boy and city slicker, all saw the same movies, listened to the same radio programs, read many of the same newspapers, and hummed the same show tunes."

Jazz Music Expresses a Spirit of Joy and Revolt

J.A. Rogers

In the early twentieth century a new form of music was developing in African American communities in the United States. This new art form was jazz, which had its roots in West African music, the traditions of blues and ragtime, and even European military band music. The city of New Orleans is credited as the birthplace of the earliest forms of jazz, then spelled *jass*. The new sound spread from New Orleans up the Mississippi River and eventually to the rest of the United States. By the 1920s jazz was becoming popular around the world. The rhythmic, improvisational music was condemned by many and enthusiastically welcomed by others. In the next selection, written in 1925, journalist and historian J.A. Rogers characterizes jazz as an instrument of revolt against convention and custom. He maintains that jazz is an expression of the time and that it has become "a safety valve for modern machine-ridden and convention-bound society."

Rogers immigrated to New York from Jamaica in the West Indies and became actively involved in the 1920s cultural movement known as the Harlem Renaissance. He published more than sixteen books as well as numerous articles and pamphlets focusing on the contributions of black people to society. Rogers died in 1966.

What after all is this taking new thing, that, condemned in certain quarters, enthusiastically welcomed in others, has nonchalantly gone on until it ranks with the movie and the dollar as the foremost exponent of modern Americanism? Jazz isn't music merely, it is a spirit that can express itself in almost anything. The true spirit of jazz is a joyous revolt from convention,

J.A. Rogers, "Jazz at Home," *Survey*, March 1, 1925.

custom, authority, boredom, even sorrow—from everything that would confine the soul of man and hinder its riding free on the air. The Negroes who invented it called their songs the "Blues," and they weren't capable of satire or deception. Jazz was their explosive attempt to cast off the blues and be happy, carefree happy even in the midst of sordidness and sorrow. And that is why it has been such a balm for modern ennui, and has become a safety valve for modern machine-ridden and convention-bound society. It is the revolt of the emotions against repression.

What Is Jazz?

In its elementals, jazz has always existed. It is in the Indian war-dance, the Highland fling, the Irish jig, the Cossack dance, the Spanish fandango, the Brazilian *maxixe*, the dance of the whirling dervish, the hula hula of the South Seas, the *danse du venire* [belly dance] of the Orient, the *carmagnole* [revolutionary ditty] of the French Revolution, the strains of Gypsy music, and the ragtime of the Negro. Jazz proper, however, is something more than all these. It is a release of all the suppressed emotions at once, a blowing off of the lid, as it were. It is hilarity expressing itself through pandemonium; musical fireworks.

The direct predecessor of jazz is ragtime. That both are atavistically African there is little doubt, but to what extent it is difficult to determine. In its barbaric rhythm and exuberance there is something of the bamboula, a wild, abandoned dance of the West African and the Haitian Negro, so stirringly described by the anonymous author of *Untrodden Fields of Anthropology*, or of the *ganza* [drum] ceremony so brilliantly depicted in [René] Maran's *Batouala* [the first novel about Africa by a black writer]. But jazz time is faster and more complex than African music. With its cow-bells, auto horns, calliopes, rattles, dinner gongs, kitchen utensils, cymbals, screams, crashes, clankings and monotonous rhythm it bears all the marks of a nerve-strung, strident, mechanized civilization. It is a thing of the jungles—modern man-made jungles.

Jazz Artists

Musically jazz has a great future. It is rapidly being sublimated. In the more famous jazz orchestras like those of Will Marion Cook, Paul Whiteman, [Noble] Sissle and [Eubie] Blake, Sam

New Orleans is known as the birthplace of jazz. By the 1920s, jazz music was enjoyed by people all over the world.

Stewart, Fletcher Henderson, Vincent Lopez and the Clef Club units, there are none of the vulgarities and crudities of the lowly origin or the only too prevalent cheap imitations. The pioneer work in the artistic development of jazz was done by Negro artists; it was the lead of the so-called "syncopated orchestras" of [William] Tyers and Will Marion Cook, the former playing for the Castles [Irene and Vernon] of dancing fame, and the latter touring as a concertizing orchestra in the great American centers and abroad. Because of the difficulties of financial backing, these expert combinations have had to yield ground to white orchestras of the type of the Paul Whiteman and Vincent Lopez organizations that are now demonstrating the finer possibilities of jazz music. "Jazz," says Sergei Koussevitzky, the new conductor of the Boston Symphony, "is an important contribution to modern musical literature. It has an epochal significance—it is not superficial, it is fundamental. Jazz comes from the soil, where all music has its beginning." And [conductor Leopold] Stokowski says more extendedly of it:

Jazz has come to stay because it is an expression of the times, of the breathless, energetic, superactive times in which we are living: it is useless to fight against it. Already its new vigor, its new vitality is beginning to manifest itself. . . . America's contribution to the music of the past will have the same revivifying effect as the injection of new, and in the larger sense, vulgar blood into dying aristocracy. Music will then be vulgarized in the best sense of the word, and enter more and more into the daily lives of people. . . . The Negro musicians of America are playing a great part in this change. They have an open mind, and unbiassed outlook. They are not hampered by conventions or traditions, and with their new ideas, their constant experiment, they are causing new blood to flow in the veins of music. The jazz players make their instruments do entirely new things, things finished musicians are taught to avoid. They are pathfinders into new realms.

The Jazz Spirit

Yet in spite of its present vices and vulgarizations, its sex informalities, its morally anarchic spirit, jazz has a popular mission to perform. Joy, after all, has a physical basis. Those who laugh and dance and sing are better off even in their vices than those who do not. Moreover jazz with its mocking disregard for formality is a leveler and makes for democracy. The jazz spirit, being primitive, demands more frankness and sincerity. Just as it already has done in art and music, so eventually in human relations and social manners, it will no doubt have the effect of putting more reality in life by taking some of the needless artificiality out. . . . Naturalness finds the artificial in conduct ridiculous. "[Miguel de] Cervantes smiled Spain's chivalry away," said [poet Lord] Byron. And so this new spirit of joy and spontaneity may itself play the role of reformer. Where at present it vulgarizes, with more wholesome growth in the future, it may on the contrary truly democratize. At all events jazz is rejuvenation, a recharging of the batteries of civilization with primitive new vigor. It has come to stay, and they are wise, who instead of protesting against it, try to lift and divert it into nobler channels.

The Harlem Renaissance

Steven Watson

Harlem, on New York City's Upper West Side, became the mecca of black intellectual and cultural life from 1920 until the Great Depression. This flourishing period is known today as the Harlem Renaissance. Although it was primarily a literary movement, the Harlem Renaissance was closely associated with African American music, theater, art, and politics. In this selection Steven Watson, a writer, exhibition curator, and practicing psychologist, traces the flowering of the movement. He describes the conflict Renaissance writers felt about their dual identities as writers creating "pure art" and "Negro writers" focused on exploring the struggles unique to African Americans. Watson also points out that these writers were greatly encouraged by the previous generation of African American writers, including W.E.B. DuBois, Alain Locke, and Jessie Fauset.

A scholar of the cultural history of the twentieth century, Watson is the author of *Strange Bedfellows: The First American Avant-Garde.*

W hat we now call "the Harlem Renaissance" flourished from the early 1920s until the onset of the Depression, and it was then known as "the New Negro Renaissance." African-American writing existed before these years, of course, and many authors who first found their voices during the 1920s produced significant work in the years following. But the New Negro's organized, self-conscious phase lasted less than a decade. The use of the avant-garde buzzword, "new," reflects the catholic embrace of the budding movement. In the 1910s, when one spoke of "the New Woman" or "the New Art," it signified a manifestation that blurred the boundaries between aesthetics, politics, and life style; an archetypal "New Poet" of that period embraced not only *vers libre*,[1] but cubism, the Industrial Workers of the World, free love, and bohemian dress. In like fashion, "the New Negro" movement embraced more than literature: it included race-building and image-building, jazz poetics, progressive or socialist politics, racial integration, the musical and sexual freedom of Harlem nightlife, and the pursuit of hedonism. ("Renaissance" was used only slightly less than "new" among the avant-garde, a term that expressed a cultural blooming in a young nation.)

The Literary Movement

The Harlem Renaissance was primarily a literary and intellectual movement composed of a generation of black writers born around the turn of the century. Among its best known figures were Langston Hughes, Zora Neale Hurston, Countee Cullen, Claude McKay, and Jean Toomer. They were not the first noteworthy black writers in America—for novelists Charles Waddell Chesnutt and James Weldon Johnson and dialect poet Paul Laurence Dunbar preceded them—but these younger writers constituted the first self-conscious black literary constellation in American history. The most effective strategy for race-building depended on art and literature, so a dual mission was thrust upon these writers: they were simultaneously charged with creating art and with bolstering the image of their race. Sterling Brown, a lesser-known Renaissance writer, has identified five themes animating the movement: 1) Africa as a source of race pride, 2) black American heroes, 3) racial political propaganda, 4) the black folk-tradition, and 5) candid self-revelation. Evoking these themes, the Renaissance authors produced a body of literature which was not only exemplary in itself but also paved the way for succeeding generations of black writers who invoked the Harlem Renaissance as the roots of their cultural tradition. Indispensable to the movement was a supporting cast of editors, patrons, and hostesses—both black and white—who greased the movement's operation and trained a spotlight on its accomplishments.

Adding to the visibility of the literary phenomenon were jazz

---

1. "free verse," or unrhymed verse without a consistent metrical pattern

musicians, producers of all-black revues, and Uptown bootleggers. While African-American literature—especially poetry—
drew a small readership, a much larger army responded to the
call of Harlem's night world. In the heat of that moment the New
Negro movement and Harlemania sometimes fused—and the
Harlem Renaissance is still recalled in the public imagination as
a golden era of jazz, poetry, liquor, sex, and clubs. While writers
will dominate the story told here, a diverse and powerful group
stands behind them.

"Two Warring Ideals"

The Harlem Renaissance participants did not promote a consistent aesthetic or write in a recognizably "Renaissance" style.
Their work ranged from the most conservatively crafted sonnets
to modernist verse to jazz aesthetics to documentary folklore.
Their agenda was contradictory and dualistic: their mission was
both race propaganda and "pure" art; they incorporated the high
culture of literature with the low culture of cabaret and the blues;
they forged identities as "writers" and as "Negro writers." Defin-
ing their selfhood—psychological, racial, and aesthetic—proved
pivotal to the key Harlem Renaissance figures, and their task was
made especially complex by the fact that most of their identities
were twofold.

In 1903 W.E.B. Du Bois had described the African-American
duality: "One ever feels his two-ness—an American, a Negro;
two souls, two thoughts, two unreconciled stirrings: two warring
ideals in one dark body, whose dogged strength alone keeps it
from being torn asunder." The key Renaissance figures were torn
between being black and white (Toomer), Jamaican and American (McKay), Negro and homosexual (Cullen, Wallace Thur-
man), propagandist and artist (Hughes, Cullen). How these individuals traversed the complex social-psychological-aesthetic
terrain of identity helps shape the story told here. Some of its
protagonists lived far from Harlem, and the Renaissance constituted just one pivotal chapter in their lives. But the geographical mecca and the movement provided the spiritual and social
foundation on which they built their literary careers.

The Harlem Renaissance was driven not only by its artists and
writers, of course, but also by economic and sociological forces

of the early twentieth century. It is no coincidence that the Renaissance began in the wake of World War I, thrived during Prohibition, and died with the onset of the Depression. Shaped by urbanization, emigration, and employment trends of the 1910s, Harlem flowered in the 1920s, and saw its descent into slumhood in the 1930s. . . .

The "black belt," as it was known, originally ran the urban corridor between Fifth and Seventh avenues in the low 130s. By 1914, black residents lived within a twenty-three-block area, and the numbers continued to grow during the decade, reflecting a migration from the South, where the lynching of blacks, a boll-weevil infestation, and a depressed job market made the region a decidedly inhospitable place. During this decade, Harlem became colonized not only by black residents but by the organizations of Negro society—the Masons, the Elks, the churches, the National Urban League and black nationalist groups, black newspapers, the YMCA. The black cabaret culture began in the mid-1910s with afternoon tea and cocoa accompanied by ragtime music, and pioneering Barron Wilkins transformed these sober affairs into tango teas, where one could not only watch professionals dance the tango, one could also enter the dance floor or purchase liquor nearby.

Simultaneous with the establishment of Harlem as the black mecca, political organizations proposed their strategies for race-building. Chief among them were Marcus Garvey's African nationalist movement, the Universal Negro Improvement Association, the National Association for the Advancement of Colored People, and the socialist African Blood Brotherhood.

By 1920, Harlem's borders extended from 130th Street to 145th Street, from Madison Avenue to Eighth Avenue. There was the merest beginning of black ownership (about 80 percent of 135th Street between Lenox and Seventh avenues). "The saloons were run by the Irish, the restaurants by the Greeks, the ice and fruit stands by the Italians, the grocery and haberdashery stores by the Jews," wrote Claude McKay. "The only Negro businesses, excepting barber shops, were the churches and the cabarets." Despite the paucity of economic ownership, Harlem had developed both the significant mass of residents necessary to forge an African-American identity and a number of strategies for doing so.

A New Epoch in Harlem

The World War I era ended on February 17, 1919, marking a new epoch in Harlem. On that afternoon, an all-black military band led the victorious soldiers of the 369th Infantry Regiment, known as the Hellfighters, up Fifth Avenue. Under James Reese Europe's leadership the sixty musicians had been applauded throughout the Continent for lively syncopation. Today, saluted by Governor Al Smith and William Randolph Hearst, they were marching home to Harlem in precision formation, wearing their khaki uniforms and dented tin helmets for the last time. Led by drum major Bill "Bojangles" Robinson, the band and soldiers turned west at 110th Street and headed up the home stretch of Lenox Avenue. Crossing 130th Street, their gait palpably loosened and they dropped the martial music to burst into "Here Comes My Daddy." At this point sweethearts and family members invaded the ranks, and the thousands of spectators on low Harlem rooftops tossed pennants and slouch hats into the air. The *New York Age* wrote, "The Hellfighters marched between two howling walls of humanity." Harlem's first pageant of celebration for its black heroes paved the way for the coming celebration of a different kind of Harlem hero—not the soldier on the battlefield, but the cultural nationalist in the parlor.

Forefathers and Midwives

Most avant-garde movements are fomented by the young against the old, with the forefathers representing an intractable and established enemy. The Harlem Renaissance, however, was actively nurtured by the previous generation of writers. Their support certainly reflected the fact that the existing established artists exerted little power and there was no literary tradition to cherish. Previously, a handful of black literary figures and intellectuals had operated in isolation or linked to an organization concerned with the social advancement of the race. The task of the New Negro movement was to identify and articulate a community consciousness rather than to overthrow existing institutions. The young writers that came of artistic age at the beginning of the 1920s—Cullen, McKay, Toomer, and Hughes—caught the public eye through the publications and organizations that their elders had established.

The preeminent figures in this ancestral constellation were the stern and intellectual patriarch, W.E.B. Du Bois, and the precious but steel-nerved uncle, Alain Locke. Rounding out this "family" were the nurturing matriarch, Jessie Fauset, the supportive uncle, James Weldon Johnson, and the enterprising elder brother, Charles S. Johnson. Their foresighted advocacy of young writers also provided them a means of controlling the direction of African-American literature; the forefathers hoped to judiciously measure out the Negro revolt teaspoon by teaspoon.

African-American Periodicals

During its initial phase the New Negro movement depended heavily on the periodicals of the black community, on whose pages was conducted a continuing conversation between writers and readers. Each publication represented an organization—*The Crisis* was the organ of the National Association for the Advancement of Colored People, *Opportunity* expressed the politics of the National Urban League, and the *New York Age* functioned as the mouthpiece for Booker T. Washington. Other papers, such as *The Messenger, The Emancipator*, and *The Challenge*, represented the more radical wings of the black movement. These periodicals offered the only outlets for black writers. (When Claude McKay, in 1917, became the first black American to appear in a white avant-garde literary magazine, *Seven Arts*, he used the pseudonym Eli Edwards.) Newspapers and magazines constituted the primary written record of the race, for books were too expensive to reach a broad readership.

Harlem's First Culture Czar

Any discussion of the Harlem Renaissance must begin with W.E.B. Du Bois, the towering Negro intellectual of the early twentieth century. Almost a decade before he founded a magazine, *The Crisis*, Du Bois wrote the classic work *The Souls of Black Folk*, a collection of essays that diagnosed the plight of black people in America. "The problem of the twentieth century is the problem of the color-line. . . ." It was in Du Bois's words that many future Renaissance writers first heard their race described with dignity. James Weldon Johnson, for example, declared it the most instrumental book since *Uncle Tom's Cabin*, and poet

Langston Hughes recalled, "My earliest memories of written words were those of W.E.B. Du Bois and the Bible. . . ." Claude McKay, who found the book in a Topeka public library, later exclaimed, "The book shook me like an earthquake."

The magazine that paved the way for the Renaissance, *The Crisis: A Record of the Darker Races*, was founded in November 1910. Its sponsor was the National Association for the Advancement of Colored People, but its sharp and magisterial voice was unmistakably Du Bois's. In person he presented a Brahmin hauteur, and his handsomely modeled light brown face became, as one friend noted, "a kind of invisible barrier that said, 'so far, but no farther.'" His affect was reserved for the pages of *The Crisis*, where his fiery polemics set the intellectual standards for the rising generation. The magazine's readership was large—circulation peaked at 95,000 in 1919—and largely middle class. His aspirations for the black race combined progressive race politics (African-Americans should develop their own institutions, write about their own experience, embrace pan-Africanism) and elitist uplift (Howard University, domestic propriety, Dunbar Apartments). The bloc of socially aspiring Negroes about whom Du Bois wrote was known as the Talented Tenth (and derisively termed "the dicties"). In his theory of trickle-down cultural development, Du Bois predicted, "The Talented Tenth rises and pulls all that are worthy of saving up to their vantage ground."

A social scientist and political leader, Du Bois was also Harlem's first culture czar. He espoused the classical formula that he took to be universal among his race—that Art should be earnest, beautiful, and above all didactic. "Thus all Art is propaganda and ever must be, despite the wailing of the purists," he wrote. He accounted Art to be an essential race-building tool, and he predicted that just as black music had won recognition in America, so too would Negro writers. In the spring of 1920, he sounded the inspiring call to arms: "A renaissance of American Negro literature is due; the material about us in the strange, heart-rending race tangle is rich beyond dream and only we can tell the tale and sing the song from the heart."

Nightclubs and Speakeasies

Herbert Asbury

The Eighteenth Amendment was enacted on January 16, 1920, to outlaw the sale and consumption of alcohol, ushering in the era of Prohibition. Although supporters believed Prohibition would reduce crime and poverty, the so-called "noble experiment" was a colossal failure. Illegal nightclubs and speakeasies sprang up across the nation and organized crime flourished. Some mob bosses opened plush nightclubs with exotic floor shows. In this excerpt, Herbert Asbury, a newspaperman in the 1920s, describes these establishments in New York and the criminal figures who operated them. Gangsters profiled in the selection include Dutch Schultz, Arnold Rothstein, Jack Diamond, Owney Madden, Larry Fay, and Waxey Gordon. Asbury also details the various ways the nightclubs swindled their customers.

Asbury gave up his newspaper job in 1928 and began writing books and magazine articles. Much of his work chronicles crime and religious hypocrisy. His 1927 book *The Gangs of New York* served as the basis for the 2002 movie *Gangs of New York*. Herbert Asbury died in 1963 at age seventy-three.

S oon after the Eighteenth Amendment went into effect the Brooklyn *Eagle* said editorially that "the knell of the cabaret was sounded when the specter of total abstinence stalked through the front door." Prohibition not only destroyed the cabaret as New York had known it for many years; the word itself disappeared from the popular vocabulary and was replaced by "night club." The cabaret and the night club were alike in some respects—both provided dancing and entertainment to attract customers, and both depended for profit upon the sale of a little food and a lot of liquor. But there the similarity ended. The entertainment in an old-time cabaret was usually more formal than that in a night club, and of a higher caliber in the latter, noise and gaudy decorations, to say nothing of the deadening effects of prohibition booze, covered up the shortcomings of the orchestra and the performers. Operating a cabaret before prohibition was a legitimate business, while running a night club during the dry era was, in general, a racket. As long as he obeyed the closing law and other laws and paid his license fees, with perhaps a reasonable donation to the Tammany district leader,[1] the cabaret operator had nothing to fear from the authorities. For the man who ran a night club, life was not so simple. Although he may have made proper arrangements with the politicians, the police, and the prohibition agents, and had taken care of the inspectors of the health and fire departments and the other city services, he never knew whether he would be allowed to keep his place open one day or one year, the double cross was one of the great indoor sports of the period. Moreover, he was constantly exposed to the possibility that a disappointed business rival might attempt to equalize matters with a pistol, a bomb, or a submachine gun. Consequently he got what he could while the getting was good. His motto was, "A short life and a thievish one."

Running a Night Club

There were literally hundreds of night-club operators during prohibition, and many of them made a great deal of money, for customers were plentiful and prices high. The cover charge in a place rated first-class ranged from two dollars to whatever could be extracted from the customer, or sucker, without evoking too many squawks. The price of a dinner varied, but was seldom less than four or five dollars, and in most of the resorts the food was terrible. It was not uncommon for a man who only a few years before had been accustomed to dining at Delmonico's or Churchill's or Mouquin's to burst into tears at the mere sight of a night-club meal. If a sucker ordered champagne, he got aerated cider and a bill for twenty-five dollars. For a split of ginger ale, or a small glass of orange juice, which were generally used to kill the taste and smell of bootleg hooch, he paid a dollar and a half and sometimes two dollars. A setup, consisting of ice and soda

---

1. leader of the New York County Democratic Party

or plain water, into which the customer poured his own liquor, cost from one to two dollars. A fifth of whiskey, so called, which might contain anything from wood alcohol to embalming fluid, was twenty dollars. As soon as the sucker got drunk, which was usually after the second slug of raw booze had ripped down his throat, the official schedule of prices went out the window; thereafter the waiters used their own judgment and charged whatever the traffic would bear.

Clip Joints

One of the most profitable branches of the night club-business was the "clip joint," which for downright viciousness was equaled only by the worst of the old-time saloons. These fragrant dives were usually hidden away in a side street, although occasionally the police found one in a Broadway basement. The typical clip joint was staffed by a bartender, two or three waiters who doubled as strong-arm men, a tough floor manager, a singer and a piano player, a half-naked cigarette girl, and from two to ten hostesses, depending upon the size of the place. The sucker was usually brought to the clip joint by a taxi driver or sent there by a hotel clerk; he was assured that he would find girls galore and lots of good liquor "right off the boat."

When he arrived he was immediately importuned to buy drinks for one or more of the hostesses, who intimated that they would be available for more interesting activities "after we get through work." The girls usually drank "gin highballs," which were compounded of water and a little orange juice or ginger ale, and for which the sucker was charged from one to two dollars. The sucker himself, for his initial drink, was given a double slug of raw alcohol doctored to resemble whiskey. If he got helplessly drunk, he was simply robbed and dumped into the gutter a block or so away from the clip joint. If through some miracle he remained fairly sober and showed a disposition to quit spending, the usual procedure was for one of the hostesses to accuse him of insulting her. Thereupon the floor manager would indignantly tell him to leave and present him with a bill, an outrageous compilation which included a large cover charge, a dozen drinks he hadn't ordered, all those he had already paid for, a bottle or two of liquor, a half dozen packs of cigarettes at a dollar each, and extras. If he paid, he was permitted to depart, although he was lucky if a sympathetic hostess didn't pick his pocket before he reached the door. If he protested, he was kicked and slugged until he was groggy or unconscious, after which he was robbed and thrown out. The police seldom raided a politically protected night club—that unpopular chore was generally performed by the federal agents—but when they did, the assignment was carried out in a very genteel and considerate manner. But the clip joints had few friends, and the police were pretty rough with them. When a victim complained about one of these dives, and could remember the address, the cops simply wrecked the joint and beat up every member of the staff they could catch. They sent a lot of clip-joint operators and strong-arm men to the hospitals, but brought very few into court.

Gangsters Take Over

The restaurant and cabaret operators who dominated New York's night life before prohibition—George Rector, the Delmonicos, Louis Sherry, the Bustaneby brothers, Captain James Churchill, the Shanleys, Thomas Healey, Jack Dunstan, Joel Rinaldo, John Reisenweber, and others—were men of standing and integrity. The night-club and clip-joint entrepreneurs who succeeded them, and whose operations invested Broadway with its "new moral tone," were of an entirely different stamp. Occasionally an honest but misguided promoter would attempt to open a night club, but since it was impossible to operate profitably without liquor, he had to begin by making an illegal connection with a bootleg ring. That meant paying off the politicians, the police, and all the others, and he soon found himself deeply involved in a situation which he couldn't handle. Invariably he either went bankrupt or was frozen out, which is a way of saying that gangsters muscled in, if he had a good location, and told him to get out or get killed.

Big-Shot Criminals

Throughout the fourteen years of prohibition, which the Anti-Saloon League had hailed joyfully as "an era of clear thinking and clean living," and for several years afterward, virtually all of New York's best-known drinking and dancing resorts were dominated by big-shot criminals. These men controlled the flow of liquor into the metropolis and managed its distribution and sale; they operated or financed night clubs partly to provide good outlets for their booze and partly for reasons of vanity. They were the real top-drawer crooks of the period; they ran the whole criminal setup in New York, and their alliances, especially in liquor, extended northward to Chicago and Detroit, southward to New Orleans and Miami, and westward to Los Angeles and San Francisco. Among other things, they planned and directed the New York liquor wars in which a thousand gangsters and bootleggers were killed. The gunmen who handled these murders, which to them were just so many jobs, never received as much publicity as their colleagues in Chicago, nor did they reach the heights of cruelty achieved by the killers who followed the banners of Johnny Torrio, Al Capone, and Dion O'Banion. Nevertheless they frequently displayed considerable imagination, and are said to have invented many of the methods used with such spectacular success in Chicago, Detroit, and elsewhere.

Nearly all of the underworld luminaries who looked upon such murders as legitimate ways to handle competition owed their eminence to the Eighteenth Amendment. They included some of the most vicious thugs and racketeers that New York has ever produced. The most powerful of the lot was Arnold Rothstein, a sure-thing gambler, and, reputedly, a fixer of prize fights, horse races, and other sporting events. His greatest achievement in this field, the details of which didn't become generally known until after his death, was rigging the 1919 World Series, which resulted in baseball's greatest scandal. Rothstein was pre-eminent in such undertakings, but actually they were just the frosting on the cake. The real source of his power was his huge bank roll. He was the underworld's big money man and backer of shady enterprises. Rothstein had money in more than a score of New York night clubs, including such famed resorts as the Cotton Club, the Silver Slipper, the Rendezvous, and Les Ambassadeurs, as well as in a considerable number of clip joints and ordinary speakeasies. He also backed an occasional musical show in the legitimate theater, and invested large sums in race horses, gambling houses, hotels, judges, politicians, policemen, and other properties which appealed to his sense of possession or were useful to him in his business. When Rothstein financed an underworld project he always received a high rate of interest, his money back, and an exorbitant share of the profits. And whoever owed Rothstein paid him, in one way or another. He retained half a dozen skilled and unscrupulous lawyers to handle the legal aspects of his transactions—he frequently operated under cover of a corporate organization. Rothstein was at the peak of his career when he was shot in the Park Central Hotel on November 5, 1928. He lived for two days, but failed to disclose the name of his murderer, who was never found, or, at least, never arrested.

Jack Diamond, Dutch Schultz, Charley Luciano, Lepke Buchalter, Bugsy Siegel, Jake Gurrah Shapiro, and Meyer Lansky, together with many others whose names were less familiar, all helped finance night clubs at various times, and provided gunmen to protect the resorts in which they were interested and to discourage rivals with whom they were at war. (A classic example of discouragement occurred on July 13, 1929, when Jack Diamond put the Hotsy Totsy Club out of business by shooting down two of its owners on a crowded dance floor.) Their main interests, however, were in rumrunning and bootlegging, and in the related fields of murder, hijacking, narcotics, prostitution, crooked gambling, racketeering, robbery, and extortion. The only one of this group who invested heavily in the night-club business was Arthur Flegenheimer, better known as Dutch Schultz, who was the beer baron of the Bronx and boss of the numbers or policy racket. His principal partner and protector in the latter enterprise was James J. Hines, a well-known Tammany politician who was sent to prison in 1939.

The Night-Club Business

During the final years of prohibition Schultz owned the Embassy Club, a very plush night spot which catered to the high-class, or Park Avenue, trade. In return for paying exorbitant prices for poor food and bad liquor, which did them little harm, the Park Avenuers rubbed elbows with top-flight gangsters, which thrilled them, and listened to the singing of Helen Morgan, Morton Downey, and the Yacht Club Boys, which amused them. Dutch Schultz was also distinguished in the underworld as the first employer of Vincent Coll, the so-called "mad dog of gangland," who was probably the most brutal killer of his time, at least in New

York. Coll loved to kill, and did so on the slightest provocation. He put several notches on his gun during a war with the Jack Diamond gang, but later broke with Schultz, organized his own mob, and began hijacking his former boss's liquor trucks. Schultz immediately offered to pay fifty thousand dollars to any man who would kill Coll, and every free-lance gunman in New York went on the prowl, eager to earn the money. On the night of February 7, 1932, one of Schultz's own killers trapped Coll in a telephone booth in a drugstore on West Twenty-third Street, near Ninth Avenue, and poured fifty bullets from a submachine gun through the glass doors. Most of the slugs lodged in Coll's body between the head and the knees. The mad dog had just passed his twenty-third birthday.

In the night-club business, the biggest of the big shots, besides Rothstein, were Owney Madden, Larry Fay; Frankie Marlow, whose real name was Gandolfo Civito; and Waxey Gordon, born Irving Wexler. The second to retire from New York's night life, after Rothstein, was Marlow, his departure being effected by the usual burst of gunfire. Marlow started as a gunman on the staff of Francesco Uale, better known as Frankie Yale, the big liquor and racketeering boss of Brooklyn, whose activities were centered in the Gowanus and Coney Island sections. One of Yale's properties at Coney Island was the Harvard Inn, which he had opened several years before prohibition, and where a young man named Alphonse Capone began his career as a dishwasher. Yale was one of the first to bring liquor into New York from the rum fleet off the coast, and in these operations Marlow was his right-hand man and chief killer. Within two or three years Marlow's share of the proceeds amounted to a fair-sized fortune, so he left Brooklyn and moved to Manhattan, where for several years he was a prominent figure in Broadway and sporting circles as well as in the liquor racket. During the middle 1920s he controlled the sale of all beer sold in Manhattan between Harlem and Forty-second Street. He also owned race horses and prize fighters, a gambling house or two, and had shares in the Silver Slipper, the Rendezvous, and other night clubs, including a vicious dive called the Club La Vie. He also owned a sizable interest in Les Ambassadeurs, and once threatened to sell out unless the name was changed to something he could spell, or at least pronounce.

Captains of the Underworld

It was common gossip in the underworld that Frankie Yale had provided the money for some of Marlow's night-club ventures, although as far as was publicly known Yale confined his operations to Brooklyn, with an occasional trip to Chicago to do a job of killing for his old friends Johnny Torrio and Al Capone. When Yale was murdered in 1928, Marlow owed him forty thousand dollars, and when pressed for payment by Yale's successor, Little Augie Carfano, insisted that Yale's death had canceled the debt. Less than a year later, on June 24, 1929, Marlow was lured from a New York night club by several of his old Brooklyn pals, and taken for the customary ride, with death at the end of the journey. His body, full of bullets, was found by motorists under a bush near a graveyard in Queens Borough, on Long Island. In his pockets were seventeen dollars in cash, a pawn ticket for a diamond ring, and a pistol permit signed by a justice of the New York Supreme Court.

Owney Madden became captain of the Old Gopher gang in 1910, when he was eighteen years old, and as such was lord of the Hell's Kitchen section of New York's lower west side. Four years later, proudly bearing the sobriquet of "Owney the Killer," and suspected by the police of five murders, Madden was convicted of complicity in a gang killing and sent to Sing Sing [prison] to serve from ten to twenty years. He was released in 1923, and so missed some three years of the golden era. He came along rapidly, however, and within a year or two had made a big name for himself as a gunman, a bootlegger, a hijacker, and as a strong-arm man in clip joints. In common with many other big shots, he was interested in the Silver Slipper, and was also associated with Rothstein in the Cotton Club and other resorts. Before he retired in the middle 1930s, Madden had been arrested fifty-seven times, on charges ranging from homicide to stealing. His record, however, shows only two convictions—the one in 1914 and another for violating a traffic ordinance. He always managed to know the right people.

And so did Waxey Gordon until 1933, when the government, unable to do anything about his more serious crimes, sent him to prison for income-tax evasion. Before the Eighteenth Amendment gave him his big chance, Gordon was a pickpocket, a sneak thief, and a small-time peddler of narcotics. He immediately went into the liquor business, and within half a dozen years was head of a big bootleg ring which imported fine whiskeys from Nova Scotia and the Bahamas. Gordon sold a little of this good liquor to selected customers at from two to four times the usual price, but most of it was cut and recut and doctored and colored until by the time it reached the ultimate consumer it was the same terrible stuff that was available everywhere. Gordon was a very rich man during the late 1920s and the early 1930s. He owned several hotels in midtown Manhattan, including the popular Piccadilly; a brewery, a distillery, a line of seagoing rum ships, a luxurious summer home in New Jersey, half a dozen expensive automobiles, handfuls of diamonds and other jewelry, a wardrobe that had cost him many thousands of dollars—he was a noted dandy—and of course, share in half a dozen night clubs.

Gangster Larry Fay

Larry Fay was a gangster and rumrunner, and a partner of James J. Hines, in a profitable racket by which small milk producers were shaken down for protection money. His police record, as published in the New York *Herald Tribune*, filled half a column of small type. Aside from all this, he possessed three distinctions—he named some of his night clubs after himself, he financed most of them with his own money, and he was the first of the big shots to become an important figure in the business. He was a little man, long-jawed and decidedly unhandsome, and he had an abiding passion for flashy clothing; he is said to have started the fashion of wearing solid-color shirts—his favorite was a violent indigo blue—with loud neckties and expensive suits. Fay's habiliments were always the best that money could buy, and many of his topcoats, suits, shoes, and shirts were made in England. When he returned from a trip to Europe in 1923 he brought twelve trunks filled with Bond Street creations made especially for him by London's most fashionable tailors. He knocked Broadway's eye out for months. He was always grateful for any flattering reference to his appearance; a newspaper reporter who called him the "Beau Brummel of Broadway" received a case of liquor and an invitation to eat and drink on the cuff for six months at one of Fay's clubs. However, the great man was practical; beneath his gaudy raiment he wore a bulletproof vest. Fay also disliked the term "racketeer"; he always insisted that he was a businessman, and to prove it maintained an ornate suite of offices near Columbus Circle, where he employed an extraordinarily large number of handsome secretaries and stenographers.

Until he hit a hundred-to-one shot at Belmont Park in 1918, when he was twenty-nine years old, Fay was a taxi driver and an unimportant punk-about-town. He sometimes ran with the old Hudson Duster gang on Manhattan's west side, and became friendly with a Duster Chieftain called Big Frenchy de Mange, who was afterward his partner in several night-club ventures. With the money won at the race track Fay bought several taxicabs; eventually he operated a large fleet and became so powerful in the industry that he controlled the two most profitable stands in New York—the Grand Central Terminal and the Pennsylvania Station. When prohibition changed the complexion of New York's underworld, Fay began running liquor down from Canada, using his taxicabs and several trucks which he was soon able to purchase. He was also associated, for a few years, with Big Bill Dwyer and others whose speedboats brought liquor into New York from Rum Row.

In less than two years Fay had accumulated about five hundred thousand dollars in cash, according to underworld report, and huge sums were rolling in from his taxi and liquor enterprises. His initial venture into the night-club field was early in 1921, when he financed several clip joints, said to have been the first dives of this type ever opened in New York, although they had already become fairly common in Chicago, Philadelphia, and Detroit. Also in 1921, Fay started the first of his big night clubs, Fay's Follies at Eighth Avenue and Fifty-fourth Street, the decorations of which are said to have cost seventy-five thousand dollars. The new resort was a big success, and took up so much of Fay's time and attention that in 1923, when Owney Madden got out of Sing Sing, Fay hired the ex-Gopher captain to supervise his clip-joint interests and act as a sort of foreman over the strong-arm boys and pullers-in. In 1924 Fay opened the most celebrated of his night spots, the El Fey at 107 West Forty-fifth Street, and when that was padlocked by the government he started another which he called the Del Fey. During the next several years he opened four or five others, and was one of the many partners in the Silver Slipper, the Rendezvous, the Cotton Club, Les Ambassadeurs, and the Casablanca. Fay was murdered while standing in front of the Casablanca on January 1, 1933, the first day in six months on which he had not worn his bullet-proof vest.

Queen of the Night Clubs

Fay's greatest contribution to the night life of the prohibition era was his sponsorship of one of Broadway's most celebrated figures—Mary Louise Cecelia Guinan, better known as Texas, a Waco girl who came to New York in 1922 to make her fortune. She made it, too, but apparently was unable to keep it. During a period of ten months in the middle 1920s Texas Guinan is said to have banked seven hundred thousand dollars, but when she died on November 5, 1933, at Vancouver, B.C., where she had been appearing with a troupe of dancing girls, she left a net estate of $28,173. She was forty-nine years old. Texas Guinan's first appearance in New York was as a substitute singer at the Café des Beaux Arts, which had been reopened as a night club after the retirement of André Bustanoby. Her singing voice never amounted to much, and she was a very poor actress, as she afterward proved when she played several parts in the legitimate theater, but she had a remarkable personality that was made to order for the noise and excitement of a night club. She was such a big hit that the operator of the Beaux Arts immediately hired her as mistress of ceremonies. Larry Fay engaged her for El Fey soon after that resort opened, and later she appeared at the Rendezvous. During the next half dozen years she operated several clubs of her own, among them the 300 Club, the Argonaut, the Century, the Salon Royal, the Club Intime, and two or three Texas Guinan Clubs, some of which were believed to have been backed by Arnold Rothstein. All of her places were frequently raided, and several were padlocked. Texas Guinan herself was often arrested, but she never went to jail, and she was never even in court for more than a few hours. Chester P. Mills, who was prohibition administrator of the New York district during the middle 1920s, wrote in *Collier's Weekly* for September 17, 1927, "I spent many wakeful hours trying to bring into camp such persons as Texas Guinan . . . who finally eluded our men with the aid of shrewd lawyers."

At the peak of her career Texas Guinan was by far the loudest noise on Broadway, and with the possible exception of Helen Morgan was the most popular night-club attraction New York had ever seen; the crowds loved her brashness and the atmosphere of excitement which surrounded her everywhere she went. Only one rival ever tried to usurp her title as Queen of the Night Clubs—an aging dame named Belle Livingston, who away back in the early 1890s was a Broadway show girl known as the Kansas Sunshine Baby. Belle Livingston opened three clubs in the late 1920s and the early 1930s, but was not very successful; she talked too much and was inclined to fight the prohibition agents instead of appealing to their better natures. Her best-known resort was the Fifty-eighth Street Country Club, a big place of five floors with bars, grills, private rooms, ping-pong games, and a miniature golf course. Belle Livingston was a big woman, some six feet tall and weighing about one hundred seventy-five pounds, and usually acted as her own bouncer. She tried to bounce a squad of enforcement agents who raided one of her clubs in 1931, and was herself bounced into jail for thirty days.

Belle Livingston has long been forgotten, but as long as there is a Broadway, Texas Guinan will be remembered for the famous wisecrack, "Hello, Sucker," with which she greeted visitors to her clubs; and for half a dozen other phrases which are still part of the nightclub and underworld argot. One night at the Rendezvous an enthusiastic sucker paid the cover charge for everybody present and grandly presented to each performer a fifty-dollar bill, whereupon Texas Guinan hauled him under a spotlight and introduced him as "a big butter-and-egg man." The name of this character has not been preserved, but as a type he was immortalized in a successful play by George S. Kaufman. On another occasion, when a singer had given her best to scattering applause, Texas Guinan shouted, "Give this little girl a great big hand." This cry is still used by masters of ceremonies to stimulate enthusiasm for their favorites, and the injunction is nearly always obeyed by docile night-clubbers. Once, however, it boomeranged, and the usually jovial Texas Guinan became furiously angry. During a raid a prohibition agent placed a paternal hand on her shoulder and called to a colleague: "Give this little girl a great big handcuff!"

The Glamour of Motion Pictures

Anonymous

Between 1910 and 1920 movies began to capture the interest of the nation. It was in the 1920s, however, that the film industry truly flourished. By the end of the decade twenty Hollywood studios had been created and were releasing an average of eight hundred films a year (which is remarkable considering that it is rare today that production exceeds five hundred films a year). The motion picture industry produced adventure films, romances, and epics, with stars including Douglas Fairbanks and Joan Crawford. Young women across America were enticed by the glamour of the silver screen and followed the fashions of their favorite actresses. In this selection an unnamed twenty-two-year-old college senior discusses her love of movies and their impact on her life with the well-known sociologist and author Herbert Blumer.

M y real interest in motion pictures showed itself when I was in about fourth grade at grammar school. There was a theater on the route by which I went home from school and as the picture changed every other day I used to spend the majority of my time there. A gang of us little tots went regularly.

One day I went to see Viola Dana in *The Five Dollar Baby*. The scenes which showed her as a baby fascinated me so that I stayed to see it over four times. I forgot home, dinner, and everything. About eight o'clock mother came after me—frantically searching the theater.

Next to pictures about children, I loved serials and pie-throwing comedies, not to say cowboy 'n' Indian stories. These kind I liked until I was twelve or thirteen; then I lost interest in that type, and the spectacular, beautifully decorated scenes took my eye. Stories of dancers and stage life I loved. Next, mystery plays thrilled me and one never slipped by me. At fifteen I liked stories of modern youth; the gorgeous clothes and settings facinated me.

Anonymous, "Motion Picture Autobiography," *Movies and Conduct*, edited by Herbert Blumer. New York, 1933.

Favorite Stars

My first favorite was Norma Talmadge. I liked her because I saw her in a picture where she wore ruffly hoop-skirts which greatly attracted me. My favorites have always been among the women; the only men stars I've ever been interested in are Tom Mix, Doug Fairbanks and Thomas Meighan, also Doug McLean and Bill Haines. Colleen Moore I liked for a while, but now her hair-cut annoys me. My present favorites are rather numerous: Joan Crawford, Billie Dove, Sue Carol, Louise Brooks, and Norma Shearer. I nearly forgot about Barbara LaMar. I really worshiped her. I can remember how I diligently tried to draw every gown she wore on the screen and how broken-hearted I was when she died. You would have thought my best friend had passed away.

Why I like my favorites? I like Joan Crawford because she is so modern, so young, and so vivacious! Billie Dove is so beautifully beautiful that she just gets under your skin. She is the most beautiful woman on the screen! Sue Carol is cute 'n' peppy. Louise Brooks has her assets, those being legs 'n' a clever hair-cut. Norma Shearer wears the kind of clothes I like and is a clever actress.

I nearly always have gone and yet go to the theater with someone. I hate to go alone as it is more enjoyable to have someone to discuss the picture with. Now I go with a bunch of girls or on a date with girls and boys or with one fellow.

The day-dreams instigated by the movies consist of clothes, ideas on furnishings, and manners. I don't day-dream much. I am more concerned with materialistic things and realisms. Nevertheless it is hard for any girl not to imagine herself cuddled up in some voluptuous ermine wrap, etc.

The influence of movies on my play as a child—all that I remember is that we immediately enacted the parts interesting us most. And for weeks I would attempt to do what that character would have done until we saw another movie and some other hero or heroine won us over.

Deeply Moved by Movies

I'm always at the mercy of the actor at a movie. I feel nearly every emotion he portrays and forget that anything else is on earth. I was so horrified during *The Phantom of the Opera* when Lon Chaney removed his mask, revealing that hideous face, that until my last day I shall never forget it.

I am deeply impressed, however, by pathos [suffering] and piti-fulness, if you understand. I remember one time seeing a movie about an awful fire. I was terrified by the reality of it and for sev-eral nights I was afraid to go to sleep for fear of a fire and even placed my hat and coat near by in case it was necessary to make a hasty exit. Pictures of robbery and floods have affected my be-havior the same way. Have I ever cried at pictures? Cried! I've practically dissolved myself many a time. How people can witness a heart-rending picture and not weep buckets of tears is more than I can understand. *The Singing Fool, The Iron Mask, Seventh Heaven, Our Dancing Daughters,* and other pictures I saw when very young which centered about the death of someone's baby and showed how the big sister insisted on her jazz 'n' whoopee re-gardless of the baby or not—these nearly killed me. Something like that, anyway; and I hated that girl so I wanted to walk up to the screen and tear her up! As for liking to cry—why, I never thought of that. It isn't a matter of liking or not. Sometimes it just can't be helped. Movies do change my moods, but they never last long. I'm off on something else before I know it. If I see a dull or morose show, it sort of deadens me and the vim and vigor dies out 'til the movie is forgotten. For example, Mary Pickford's movie—*Sparrows*—gave me the blues for a week or so, as did li'l Sonny Boy in *The Singing Fool.* The poor kid's a joke now.

This modern knee-jiggling, hand-clapping effect used for ac-companying popular music has been imitated from the movies, I think. But unless I've unconsciously picked up little manner-isms, I can think of no one that I've tried to imitate.

Learning About Love

Goodness knows, you learn plenty about love from the movies. That's their long run; you learn more from actual experience, though! You do see how the gold-digger systematically gets the poor fish in tow. You see how the sleek-haired, long-earringed, languid-eyed siren lands the men. You meet the flapper, the good girl, 'n' all the feminine types and their little tricks of the trade. We pick up their snappy comebacks which are most handy when dispensing with an unwanted suitor, a too ardent one, too back-ward one, etc. And believe me, they observe and remember, too.

I can remember when we all nudged one another and giggled at the last close-up in a movie. I recall when during the same sort of close-up when the boy friend squeezes your arm and looks soulfully at you. Oh, it's lotsa fun! No, I never fell in love with my movie idol. When I don't know a person really, when I know I'll never have a chance with 'em, I don't bother pining away over them and writing them idiotic letters as some girls I've known do. I have imagined playing with a movie hero many times though; that is while I'm watching the picture. I forget about it when I'm outside the theater. Buddy Rogers and Rudy Valentino have kissed me oodles of times, but they don't know it. God bless 'em!

Yes, love scenes have thrilled me and have made me more receptive to love. I was going with a fellow whom I liked as a playmate, so to speak; he was a little younger than me and he liked me a great deal. We went to the movie—Billie Dove in it. Oh, I can't recall the name but Antonio Moreno was the lead, and there were some lovely scenes which just got me all hot 'n' bothered. After the movie we went for a ride 'n' parked along the lake; it was a gorgeous night. Well, I just melted (as it were) in his arms, making him believe I loved him, which I didn't. I sort of came to, but I promised to go steady with him. I went with him 'til I couldn't bear the sight of him. Such trouble I had trying to get rid of him, and yet not hurt his feelings, as I had led him to believe I cared more than I did. I've wished many times that we'd never seen the movie. Another thing not exactly on the subject but important, I began smoking after watching Dolores Costello, I believe it was, smoke, which hasn't added any joy to my parents' lives.

A Nation at Play

Stuart Chase

Author Stuart Chase earned international acclaim as an innovator in consumer protection, a promoter of public education, and an activist for responsive government and ecological concerns. He advised presidents and interpreted contemporary issues in thirty-five books and hundreds of articles. In the following selection published in 1928, Chase examines the leisure activities that people enjoyed during his era. He notes that play is a "vital principle" in the growth of children and a "major necessity" in the life of adults. He emphasizes that the most rewarding forms of play are those that require active participation, including sports and dancing. In the machine age, people are becoming more passive, Chase argues, spending their leisure time listening to the radio or watching sports instead of engaging in more demanding pastimes. Chase also describes the development of what he calls "mass produced amusements"—entertainment intended to be enjoyed by thousands of people, including motion pictures, magazines, and sporting events. He concludes that the country needs to focus on developing new forms of recreation that require more direct involvement and therefore create deeper satisfaction. Stuart Chase died in 1985 at the age of ninety-seven.

In a jungle clearing, a low brushwood fire is burning. About the fire a score of naked human beings are stretched upon the ground. Over the top of the black belt of encircling trees comes the full moon. Suddenly a man begins to sing, a deep, full-throated chant. The loungers leap to their feet and join the song. Singing, they begin to dance. It is a weird wild dance, involving every muscle of the body. They strike their thighs with their hands—in lieu of the musical instruments which they have never invented. The rhythm moves ever faster to a leaping climax. Each man is rapt, intense, dancing his own dance, yet there is a rough unity and form in the whole group. The climax reached, the

Stuart Chase, "Play," *Whither Mankind: A Panorama of Modern Civilization,* edited by Charles A. Beard. Freeport, NY: Books for Libraries Press, 1928.

dancers fall exhausted to the ground, panting, glistening with sweat, spent and satisfied.

This, according to the reporting anthropologist, is a favorite form of play among the Rock Veddahs of Ceylon—one of the most primitive of surviving nature peoples. The dance is connected with exorcism against wild beasts, but it is also a profound expression of personal impulse and desire. Muscles, voice, rhythm, senses are all involved. It is the vital principle of raw life at the full. If we would understand play, we must begin in some such jungle clearing. It is our base line.

From Ceylon we move to the most civilized city which ever the hands of man have built [Athens]. [The Greek philosopher] Plato tells us of the philosophy of play in that city. "The mere athlete becomes too much of a savage, and the mere musician is melted and softened beyond what is good for him. . . . The two should therefore be blended in right proportions." The Athenian ideal of citizen was artist, athlete, soldier, statesman, and philosopher, all in one. A reasonably full order, but the Acropolis still stands to remind us of how well it was achieved. Nor must we forget that time in Hellas [Greece] was measured in units of play; the four-year intervals between the Olympic games. . . .

Play and the Machine Age

Tonight in the United States of America in the year 1928, thirty million people are in their homes listening to sounds coming out of a small polished box. Wrapt and motionless they sit. Anon someone turns a knob and the rhythm of the sound changes, but its eternal monotonousness never changes, save when it suddenly up-rushes into a voice like that of a very large and very startled crow. Then somebody turns another knob and the timeless chant goes on.

Once a singer sang a song. Conceivably he enjoyed it, and so his singing was play. That song was heard by an audience, who watched the singer; watched his lips, watched his movements, caught something of his spirit, and also conceivably enjoyed it— but at one remove; the audience did not itself sing. The song meanwhile, with the utmost scientific ingenuity, was inscribed upon a plate of composition material, and by running a sharp instrument over that material it could be reproduced, and still enjoyed—at two removes from reality. The plate and the sharp instrument are finally set down in front of a radio broadcaster. Not thirty million people, but a solid fraction of them, are, as they turn the knobs, listening to a song which one machine has caught from another machine, which was caught, lidless and blind, by the first machine from a more or less bored singer vocalizing into its dead and impersonal face. And those of us who hear this song, while we are indeed "playing" the radio, are not playing as the Rock Veddahs, and the Athenians, define the term. We are not playing ourselves; we are being played to—and at three removes from the original source.

Among Western peoples—particularly those which had adopted the Puritan way of life—play was not in high repute at the beginning of the machine age. In America, with a stubborn continent to conquer, this was especially true. Unremitting labor was the price of survival. . . .

What is play; is it an instinct to begin with? The latter is still a matter for acrimonious debate between the behaviorists and the more orthodox psychologists, and thus scientifically unanswerable. But there seems to be a pretty general consensus of opinion among those who have been concerned with the behavior of mankind, that play is a vital principle in the growth of children, and ranks as a major necessity, not far below hunger and mating, in the life of the adult. Furthermore with the comings of the machine, and particularly in the United States of America, the age-long biological balance is threatened by monotonies and muscular repressions in work which give play an unprecedented significance. Increasingly it becomes the flywheel of modern life. "There is nothing in our inheritance which savors of factory, treadmill, or office stool. We must acquire these priceless habits, and often at the loss of our entire inheritance which included freedom to fight or run, or everlastingly to fool around. Life hates monotony but loves rhythm—in heart beat, in intestinal contraction, in poetry, music, play." Which, from Mr. [Jimmy] Dorsey, brings us not so far from the clearing in the jungle.

The Value of Play

The most rewarding forms, of play furthermore, are those in which the player participates directly with his own muscles, his own voice, his own rhythm. To exercise the faculty vicariously through the play of others, while frequently amusing enough, is far less helpful biologically. In brief, first hand is better than second hand.

If this distinction is a valid one, it follows that the value of play in a given culture may be roughly appraised by the volume of its participating as against its non-participating forms. A group given to doing is on the whole having more fun, and serving its nervous system better, than a group given to watching.

We have in the Western World a costly and stupendous organization of recreation and amusement. How much are we as citizens of that world getting out of it? Is it really providing us with fun, with release, with something of the satisfaction which the Rock Veddahs and the Greeks have known? No conclusive answer to this basic question will be found in this paper. An adequate appraisal would require months, nay years, of patient research. I can only sketch the barest introduction to the problem.

Extent and Forms of Play

An initial step is obviously to secure some idea of the extent and of the specific forms of play now practised among Western peoples. The following table is an attempt to do this for the United States—the nation which is undoubtedly the outstanding exhibit of the machine age, and the type toward which other Western peoples, for good or for ill, are at present drifting. Nobody, so far as I can learn, has tried to construct a similar table, and accordingly it can only be regarded with the charity which a pioneering effort deserves.

Estimated Annual Cost of Play in America

Forms impossible without machinery

Pleasure motoring (⅔ of total cost)	$ 5,000,000,000
Vacations and travel (Transportation element primarily)	2,000,000,000
Moving pictures	1,500,000,000
Newspapers, tabloids, light fiction (in part)	1,000,000,000
Radio	750,000,000
Phonographs, pianolas, etc.	250,000,000
Telephone—pleasure factor only	100,000,000
Flying, bicycling, etc.—pleasure factor	25,000,000
Total	*$10,625,000,000*

Forms conceivable without machinery

Entertaining, visiting, night clubs, road houses—
(food and service factor). 3,000,000,000
Candy, chewing gum, hard and soft drinks—
(in part only) 2,000,000,000
Tobacco—(in part) 1,500,000,000
Collections, hobbies, pets. 1,000,000,000
Shows, theatres, concerts, religious revivals,
lectures, etc. 500,000,000
Gifts (in part). 500,000,000
Golf. 500,000,000
Social clubs (upkeep factor only) 250,000,000
Children's toys. 250,000,000
Indoor games—cards, billiards, pool, chess, etc.. . . 100,000,000
Playgrounds, camping, hiking 100,000,000
Dancing, jazz palaces, etc. 100,000,000
Amusement parks 100,000,000
Processions, celebrations, pageants. 50,000,000
Swimming and bathing beaches 50,000,000
Musical instruments (non-automatic). 50,000,000
Hunting and fishing 50,000,000
Gambling, including stock exchanges—
(commission element only). 50,000,000
Horse-racing 50,000,000
Football 50,000,000
Baseball 50,000,000
Sport clothes 50,000,000
Prize fighting. 15,000,000
Tennis and allied games. 15,000,000
Yachting and boating 10,000,000
Field sports 10,000,000
Winter sports. 10,000,000
Indoor sports—gymnasiums, basketball, bowling,
etc. 10,000,000

Grand total, all forms $21,045,000,000

How Do Children Play in the Machine Age?

. . . How do children play in the machine age? From many points
of view this is the most important question of all. Fortunately
there is a very careful statistical study available in this connection—though somewhat limited in area. Messrs. [H.C.] Lehman
and [P.A.] Witty have tabulated the frequency of play forms

among some 7,000 school children and young people, both urban and rural, in Kansas. They drew up a list of 200 common methods of play, and had each child grade frequencies on the list, and also note other forms not given on the list. (Altogether, over 800 forms of play were noted and tabulated.) The outstanding results of this inquiry, conducted at intervals in 1923, 1924, and 1926, may be summarized as follows:

Most Frequent Play Forms

Boys and Young Men
[Numbered in order of frequency]

	8 Years Old	12 Years Old	15 Years Old	18 Years Old
1.	Funny papers	Funny papers	Funny papers	Reading newspapers
2.	Reading	Reading	Reading	Funny papers
3.	Playing catch	Playing catch	Playing catch	Automobiling
4.	Drawing	Automobiling	Automobiling	Movies
5.	Romping	Movies	Movies	Watching sports
6.	Gathering flowers	Playing baseball	Baseball	Playing catch
7.	Cutting with scissors	Playing football	Watching sports	Baseball
8.	Listening to stories	Bicycling	Football	Reading books
9.	Carpentry work	Wrestling	Radio	Football
10.	Playing football	Carpentry	Basketball	Driving motor
11.	Automobiling	Watching sports	Wrestling	Radio
12.	Phonograph	Radio	Bicycling	Basketball

Girls and Young Women

	8 Years Old	15 Years Old	22 Years Old
1.	Funny papers	Funny papers	Reading newspapers
2.	Reading	Reading	Writing letters
3.	Skipping rope	Automobiling	Visiting
4.	Drawing	Playing piano	Going to shows
5.	Scissors work	Movies	Automobiling
6.	"Just singing"	Writing letters	Reading books and magazines
7.	Looking at pictures	Phonograph	Dancing
8.	Dolls	Visiting	Movies

9. Playing house	Gathering flowers	Strolling
10. Listening to stories	Singing	Phonograph
11. Gathering flowers	Teasing somebody	Social clubs
12. Playing piano	Looking at pictures	Playing piano

The astonishing hold of the "funnies" needs no comment. One suspects that Kansas—primarily an agricultural state—is not unique in this regard. I can see no great evil in the funny papers; I can only see many other things which are conceivably more fun if the modern child had free access to them.

Indeed the children were asked in this same study to name what they would like best to play. For boys from 8 to 15, popularity ran to participating games—football, baseball, basketball, boxing, horseback riding. The funny papers came *eleventh* on the list. It would appear, accordingly, that Kansas children, at least, have not the space and equipment to play what they like the best. The newspapers, on the other hand, are always there. They constitute father's chief recreation as well. Furthermore, win this popularity grading, second-hand play forms—motors, movies, radio, watching sports, all tended to come *after* specific participating games. The boy seems to know his needs better than his world knows them.

Whatever else the patient researches of Messrs. Lehman and Witty show, they prove, beyond all peradventure, the hold of mechanized forms on the play of children, even as we have traced it in the recreation of adults. The eight-year-olds were the freest both of machinery and commercial exploitation, but these forces tramped down upon them relentlessly as they aged. . . .

Mass-Produced Amusement

Finally, the machine age has given us mass production in amusement, run according to up-to-date business methods. We have been "sold" on play precisely as we have been sold on tooth powder, bathtubs, snappy suits and electrical refrigerators. Motors, bicycles (presently aeroplanes), baseball, moving pictures, Broadway, night clubs, college football, prize fights, Coney Islands, radios, victrolas, lecture bureaus, tabloids, confession magazines, best sellers, horse-racing, travel bureaus, plus fours, revival meetings, Boy Scouts, cigarettes, antique furniture—all have gone into quantity production, following accepted formulæ of advertising, salesmanship; the limit of price the traffic will bear, and all have proved soundly profitable, with wide margins of credit from the banks, and as often as not a listing on the stock exchange.

Prize Fighting

At the first Dempsey-Tunney fight for the heavyweight boxing championship of the world, 135,000 spectators saw the match, and they paid $2,000,000 for their seats—not counting what the speculators made. Mr. Dempsey received $750,000 for 30 minutes work, Mr. Tunney received $450,000, while the profits of Mr. Tex Rickard, the promoter, were $437,000. Mr. Rickard's Madison Square Garden voting trust certificates are listed on the New York Curb Exchange. With such profits they should be in the main tent, along with General Motors and the Radio Corporation of America. In 1850, Tom Sayers, the English boxing champion, was glad to fight 44 rounds for £5 a side. But perhaps he fought for the fun of it.

In the eighteenth century prize fighting was a sport, beloved of royalty and gentry. In the nineteenth century it became a game, deserted by the élite and controlled by the underworld. In the twentieth century it has passed into the category of big business, financed by the banks, issuing securities, and licensed by the state—like banking and insurance. In New York recently a syndicate was organized by a certain Mr. Jimmy Johnson to buy the contracts of champion boxers and leading contenders, and so happily to effect a monopoly of the whole sport. "The boxing industry (note the word industry) is reaching gigantic proportions and the time has arrived for big business methods. We propose to handle boxers in the same fashion the moving-picture producers handle their star performers." Than which nothing could be more business-like.

Sports Become Big Business

Baseball has long since entered the ranks of big business with its 20,000,000 paid admissions to the two big leagues, its million dollar world series event, and its purchasing of the contracts of players to the extent of over $2,000,000 each year. It has been judiciously calculated furthermore that Mr. Babe Ruth, the home-run batter, is worth a cool $1,000,000 a year in extra admission fees to the American League.

Football has but recently broken into the admittedly professional ranks. A certain Mr. C.C. Pyle, popularly known as "Cold Cash" Pyle, induced the famous Mr. Red Grange to leave the lists of college football and act as cornerstone for a professional league. (This is the same Mr. Pyle who started tennis as big business with the purchase of Miss Suzanne Lenglen—for $200,000.) On the day Red Grange left the amateur ranks, he cleared $375,000, with the promise of making a million before the winter was over. At the same time the use of his name was sold to a sweater manufacturer for $12,000, a shoe manufacturer for $5,000, a cap maker for $2,500, and to a cigarette company for $1,000—the latter bargain figure doubtless due to the fact that Red never smokes. A candy company sold six million "Red Grange Chocolate Bars" in thirty days, for a consideration not disclosed. During this period Red received 187 telephone calls, sixty telegrams, and thirty-nine personal visits from commercial firms eager to capitalize his name and fame.

Miss Gertrude Ederle, after swimming the English Channel, received over a million dollars worth of commercial offers, a gross even greater than Red's.

College football while amateur in name is professional in spirit, and constitutes what is known as a major industry. A good team is not only the chief claim to fame of a given college; it is also frequently its financial backbone. Its profits (running up as high as $500,000 a year in some cases) maintain all other college sports; while its success is a harbinger for endowments from rich and happy alumni. Speculators reap a magnificent reward at every big game, selling $2 tickets to prosperous butter and egg merchants for $100—more or less. Meanwhile a retired college coach declares: "I will guarantee any first-class high school player that I can get him through any one of a half a dozen good colleges with board and tuition paid and no one pressing him for payment of his 'loans' afterward." In these circumstances the suggestion of Mr. Heywood Broun that college football turn frankly professional, buying and selling its players as do the baseball leagues, seems eminently just. . . .

The Impact of New Forms of Recreation

In its broadest outline the situation seems to be this: the industrial revolution has wrenched most of us away from those manual, handicraft tasks which gave us muscular activity and a margin of true play in making and fashioning things for our own use and amusement. With these tasks have gone the old community play forms, the roof raising, the barn dance, the Maypole, the harvest festival, the sugaring off. Such often flourished in the teeth of the Puritans. Our jobs today are less active, and even when we use a set of muscles in a factory, it is all too frequently the same set day in and day out. All-round development, such as the pioneer and the craftsman knew, is increasingly a thing of the past.

Meanwhile we have more time on our hands by virtue of shorter working hours. Children—with the abatement of the old-time chores—have far more time as well. Now to use this time, and to offset the non-active or over-specialized modern job, play is necessary. Furthermore, we have more income with which to finance this new demand. A culture which encouraged us to use that time and money by substituting valuable new forms of play for the forms which had been lost would be a wise culture. But the balance sheet of modern play that we have been examining is hardly a document of unalloyed wisdom. Not knowing where to turn we have turned into the clicking turnstile—at fifty cents a click.

A fraction of the extra time and money has been devoted to new participating forms of recreation, that do indeed release the human spirit, equate the biological balance, and return as much, or more, to life as ever was lost with the passing of the handicraft era. Particularly noteworthy in this respect is the out-of-doors movement, with its new parks, playgrounds, pools, beaches, trails and camping places. Also important is the growth in international sports, the Olympic games, the Davis Cup tennis matches and others, leading to friendly rivalry among nations. And perhaps even more important in the long run is the new conception of education through play which many schools are beginning to experiment with—though the relative number of children actually touched by this philosophy to date is very small.

But a far greater amount of money, and probably of time, is devoted to forms of play which at their best do not furnish an equivalent release, and at their worst compound the harm which flows from over-mechanized daily work. Motoring, movies, second-hand thrills in sports, in tabloid crimes, and in confession magazines, the funnies, the radio, even the remorseless rhythm of jazz dancing—all are burdened with elements against which the spirit of play beats its wings in vain. . . .

What the age of machinery has given us in time, it would fain take away again by degrading the opportunities which that time affords; by standardizing our recreations on a quantity production basis, by making us watchers rather than doers, by exploiting our leisure for profit, by surfeiting us with endless mechanical things to monkey with—from gasoline cigar lighters to million dollar cruising yachts, by forcing the pace of competition in play until it turns into work, and above all by brutalizing in recreation millions of human beings who are already brutalized by the psychological imperatives of their daily labor. And it will take more barn dances than [automobile manufacturer] Henry Ford can ever pay for, to throw off the yoke of that brutality.

But who shall be the winner in another generation, only the gods can tell.

Chronology

1920

January 2: Twenty-seven hundred suspected alien dissidents are arrested under orders from Attorney General A. Mitchell Palmer.

January 5: The Boston Red Sox sell Babe Ruth to the New York Yankees for $125,000.

January 16: The Eighteenth Amendment to the U.S. Constitution goes into effect prohibiting the sale, manufacture, and transportation of alcohol. The amendment is repealed in 1933.

March 26: The novel *This Side of Paradise* by F. Scott Fitzgerald is published.

May 5: Nicola Sacco and Bartolomeo Vanzetti are arrested for the murder of a shoe factory paymaster and a guard.

August 26: The Nineteenth Amendment to the U.S. Constitution takes effect, giving women the right to vote.

October 23: *Main Street*, a novel by Sinclair Lewis featuring small town life, is published.

November 2: Republican Warren G. Harding wins the presidency of the United States.

November 25: The first live play-by-play of a football game airs on radio at College Station, Texas.

1921

February 6: Charlie Chaplin stars in the silent film comedy, *The Kid.*

March 21: The U.S. Congress approves the burial of an unknown soldier in Arlington National Cemetery.

May 19: The first law limiting immigration is passed.

September 7: The first Miss America Beauty Pageant is held in Atlantic City, New Jersey, with eight contestants.

1922

May 30: Harding accepts the Lincoln Memorial on behalf of the American people at its dedication.

July 8: Jazz trumpeter Louis Armstrong arrives in Chicago from New Orleans and joins King Oliver's band.

August 28: Radio Station WEAF in New York City broadcasts the first radio commercial.

September 22: *Tales of the Jazz Age*, a collection of short stories by F. Scott Fitzgerald, is published.

1923

March 3: The first issue of *Time* magazine is published.

March 23: The song "Yes, We Have No Bananas" is released and quickly becomes one of the most popular songs of the 1920s.

July 23: David C. Stephenson, KKK Grand Dragon of Indiana, speaks in Kokomo, Indiana, to a crowd of one hundred thousand white-robed Klansmen. He extols the virtues of white supremacy.

August 2: Harding dies, and Vice President Calvin Coolidge becomes president.

October 15: Senate hearings begin on the Teapot Dome scandal involving corrupt members of the Harding administration who were involved with secret leasing of the government's oil fields to private businesses.

October 29: A dance called the Charleston is introduced in the Broadway show *Runnin' Wild* and becomes the new dance craze.

1924

February 3: Former president Woodrow Wilson dies.

February 12: George Gershwin composes his symphonic jazz piece *Rhapsody in Blue*.

May 26: A second, more restrictive immigration law is passed.

August 5: The comic strip *Little Orphan Annie* first appears in the *Chicago Tribune*.

November 2: Coolidge wins the presidential election.

November 9: Nellie Taylor Ross of Wyoming becomes the first woman governor in the United States.

November 27: The first Macy's Thanksgiving Day Parade, with horse-drawn floats, is held in New York City.

1925

April 10: *The Great Gatsby* by F. Scott Fitzgerald is published.
July 21: A Dayton, Tennessee, jury finds John T. Scopes guilty of teaching the theory of evolution.
August 8: Forty thousand members of the Ku Klux Klan march in Washington, D.C.

1926

February 27: Chicago business leaders call on the U.S. Senate to investigate organized crime.
April 5: The U.S. Senate begins hearings on the effects of Prohibition.
April 18: Martha Graham, known as the mother of modern dance, performs her first independent concert at the Forty-Eighth Street Theater in New York.
May 9: Admiral Richard Byrd flies to the North Pole.
May 18: Evangelist Aimee McPherson disappears off the coast of California. She appears six weeks later, claiming to have been kidnapped.
June 1: *The Sun Also Rises* by Ernest Hemingway is published.
August 6: Gertrude Ederle is the first woman to swim the English Channel.
August 23: Silent film star Rudolph Valentino dies in New York City. His funeral attracts one hundred thousand mourners.

1927

April 25: A demonstration of long-distance television broadcasting is successful.
May 21: Charles Lindbergh completes the first solo flight across the Atlantic.
August 23: After many appeals, Nicola Sacco and Bartolomeo Vanzetti are executed in Massachusetts.
October 6: Al Jolson stars in *The Jazz Singer*, the first motion picture with sound.
December 20: Henry Ford unveils the Model A.
December 27: Jerome Kern's musical *Showboat* opens on Broadway.

1928

January 3: Eugene O'Neill's play *Strange Interlude* opens on Broadway.

May 23: Coolidge vetoes the McNary-Haugen farm relief bill.

June 8: Louis Armstrong records "West End Blues."

November 6: Herbert Hoover is elected president.

1929

February 14: Al Capone's mobsters carry out the St. Valentine's Day massacre in Chicago.

May 16: The first Academy of Motion Picture Arts and Sciences Awards ceremony (Academy Awards) is held.

July 20–30: Avon Foreman, age fifteen, sets the juvenile record for flagpole sitting.

August 8: The *Graf Zeppelin* airship leaves New Jersey to fly around the world. The trip takes twelve days.

September 14: Attackers kill Ella Mae Wiggins, a textile mill striker in Gastonia, North Carolina.

October 18: *Look Homeward, Angel*, a novel by Thomas Wolfe, is published.

October 23–29: The stock market crashes.

For Further Research

Books

Judith S. Baughman, ed., *American Decades, 1920–1929*. Detroit: Gale Research, 1996.

Edward Behr, *Prohibition: Thirteen Years That Changed America*. New York: Arcade, 1996.

Matthew J. Bruccoli, ed., *F. Scott Fitzgerald: A Life in Letters*. New York: Charles Scribner's Sons, 1994.

Paul A. Carter, *Another Part of the Twenties*. New York: Columbia University Press, 1973.

Sarah Jane Deutsch, *From Ballots to Breadlines: American Women, 1920–1940*. Oxford, UK: Oxford University Press, 1994.

Lynn Dumenil, *The Modern Temper: American Culture and Society in the 1920s*. New York: Hill and Wang, 1995.

Richard Wightman Fox and T.J. Lears, eds., *The Culture of Consumption: Critical Essays in American History, 1880–1980*. New York: Pantheon, 1983.

Erica Hanson, *A Cultural History of the United States Through the Decades: The 1920s*. San Diego: Lucent, 1999.

David Levering Lewis, *When Harlem Was in Vogue*. Oxford, UK: Oxford University Press, 1979.

Walter Lippmann, *A Preface to Morals*. New York: Macmillan, 1929.

Mark Sullivan, *Our Times: America at the Birth of the Twentieth Century*. New York: Charles Scribner's Sons, 1926.

Irving Werstein, *Shattered Decade, 1919–1929*. New York: Charles Scribner's Sons, 1970.

Edmund Wilson, *The Shores of Light: A Literary Chronicle of the 1920s and 1930s*. New York: Farrar, Straus and Giroux, 1952.

Web Sites

The Authentic History Center: 1920s, www.authentichistory. com/1920s.html. General images of the 1920s are featured on this site. It also includes audio and speeches of the 1920s.

Comedy Central, www.otr.com/comedy.html. This site traces the development of early radio comedy.

Jazz Moves Up River: Jazz Centers of the 1920s, www.d.umn. edu/cla/faculty/tbacig/studproj/is3099/jazzcult/20sjazz/up river.html. This site presents the influence of jazz culture upon popular culture in the 1920s. It also discusses the various aspects of the American jazz culture.

Kingwood College Library: American Cultural History, 1920–1929, http://kclibrary.nhmccd.edu/decade20.html. This site helps the user gain a broad understanding of the culture of the 1920s. It also provides links to the art and architecture of the 1920s.

Index